AF316769

STEP INTO SELF (THEORY)

The Pain That Birthed My Purpose

Copyright © 2026 Raymond Williams

DEDICATION

To my family,
who stood in that hospital room after returning from a 12-minute absence from
LIFE

and gave me a reason to come back.

• • •

To the 98.5%,

who have been performing lives that don't fit them—

this is your permission to stop.

• • •

And to the DNA-encoded purpose

that waited inside me through every wrong turn,

every borrowed identity,

and every year I spent living someone else's blueprint.

Thank you for not giving up on me.

TABLE OF CONTENTS

I lay on that ER table for twelve minutes — no heartbeat, no breath, no me. Three blood clots had found their way to my lungs. My family stood in that room and did not know if I was coming back. I did not know if I was coming back. And in those twelve minutes—on the wrong side of the line between here and gone—I was not thinking about what I had piled up.

Not the titles. Not the positions. Not the things that looked impressive on paper but felt hollow in the quiet. I was thinking about the work that only my particular design could do—the work that would not exist in the world if I chose the safe path over the real one. The contribution that was mine to make and no one else's, written into my DNA before I had any say in the matter.

I came back. And the clarity that came back with me was this: the only thing that will matter when you reach that edge—and every one of us reaches it, in one form or another—is whether you used the gift you were given. Not whether you were impressive. Not whether you were safe. Whether you were real. Whether the life you lived was the one encoded in you, or the one assigned to you by people who never knew what was inside you.

This book exists because of those twelve minutes. What follows is not a theory I borrowed from someone else's research. It was paid for with twelve minutes without breath in my body. It is the framework that came back with me from the edge— the one that has transformed thousands of lives, including my own, since then. And it begins with a number that will either wake you up or allow you to keep sleeping. The choice is yours.

CHAPTER 1: THE UNSEEN WEALTH – LIVING A LIFE ALIGNED WITH PURPOSE

The deep truth that the greatest treasures in life are freely given often escapes us in a world focused on material gain. We are flooded with messages that link success with wealth, power, and status, leading us to believe that happiness can be bought and sold. Yet, the most valuable gifts, the ones that truly feed the soul, are often the simplest, the most readily available, and entirely free.

Consider the staggering, almost unbelievable statistic that only a tiny 1 to 1.5% of people are living in alignment with their inborn, DNA-driven purpose. This truth reveals a massive field of wasted potential, a sea of unfulfilled dreams and unrealized destinies.

It raises the question: What keeps us from accepting our true selves, from pursuing the paths that align with our deepest core? What prevents us from accessing the genetic blueprint for meaning that exists within us?

Imagine the power of self-knowledge. Imagine understanding the inner workings of your own mind, knowing the unique patterns of your thoughts, actions, and reactions. Imagine having a clear understanding of your strengths and weaknesses, your drivers and signals. Imagine knowing exactly what lights your fire, what brings you genuine fulfillment and joy, and what fills your life with a deep sense of purpose—what your DNA has been trying to tell you since before you were born.

This level of self-awareness is not merely a luxury; it is a basic human need. It is the key to opening a life of meaning, a life where every action is filled with intention, and every moment is experienced with a deep sense of connection. The pursuit of this inner knowledge is a process of self-discovery, a process of peeling back the layers of cultural pressure and outside expectations to reveal the real self that lies beneath, to uncover the DNA-encoded purpose that has been waiting all along.

I know exactly how this feels because I've been there. I've lived disconnected from my DNA-encoded purpose, wondering why success felt so empty, why achieving the next goal never brought the satisfaction I expected, why I couldn't shake the feeling that I was missing something fundamental. The weight of that disconnect is heavy. It's waking up every morning and going through the motions of a life that doesn't quite fit. It's looking in the mirror and barely recognizing the person staring back because you've been playing a role for so long you've forgotten who you actually are underneath. Let me show you what I learned the hard way, what it cost me to discover, and how you can find your own path without paying the same price I did.

The Lie of Material Success

In a society that often links success with financial wealth, it's easy to fall for the lie that material things are the ultimate measure of happiness. However, the tragic reality of celebrity deaths by their own hand—Robin Williams, Anthony Bourdain, Kate Spade, Avicii, the hopelessness that troubled even the most wealthy and famous— serves as a stark reminder that money cannot buy fulfillment. These people, despite their outward success, struggled with a deep sense of emptiness, a void that could not be filled by material things, a disconnect from the purpose encoded in their very DNA.

Look around at the parade of success stories that fill our media. How many people who have achieved what society defines as "success" are genuinely fulfilled? The mansion on the hill, the luxury car in the driveway, the exclusive vacations—these are the trophies of achievement in our culture. Yet behind closed doors, many of these apparent winners in life's game are facing battles of emptiness, addiction, broken relationships, and spiritual poverty. They have climbed the ladder only to discover it was leaning against the wrong wall entirely.

Robin Williams made millions of people laugh. He had wealth most of us can't even imagine, fame that opened every door, talent that won him every award worth winning. He hung himself in his bedroom. Anthony Bourdain traveled the entire world, ate at the finest restaurants, got paid enormous amounts of money to do what most people would consider a dream job. He killed himself in a hotel room in France. Kate Spade built a fashion empire from nothing, created a brand recognized everywhere. She couldn't escape the despair that comes from living outside your DNA-driven purpose. Avicii sold out stadiums, had fans who would have done anything for him, and experienced success at a level most musicians only dream about. He ended his own life at twenty-eight years old. Twenty-eight.

Here's the pattern, the undeniable pattern that emerges when you look at these stories honestly: Money doesn't fix what's broken when you're living outside your DNA-driven purpose. The mansion with the perfect kitchen and the swimming pool can't cure the depression that comes from spending your days doing work that has nothing to do with who you actually are. The massive bank account doesn't stop the panic attacks at 3 a.m. when you're alone with your thoughts and you can't remember the last time you felt genuinely happy. All that wealth, all that success, all that external validation just makes the emptiness echo louder in the quiet moments when you can't pretend anymore.

Now look at the corporate world, the world we're told to aspire to. CEOs making eight, nine figures a year who can't sleep without pills, who wake up at 2 a.m. with their hearts racing, who haven't had a real conversation with their spouse in months. VPs who have their first heart attack at forty-five and their second one at forty-nine. Middle managers who drink themselves numb every single night because actually feeling how much they hate their lives is worse than the hangovers. They climbed every rung of the ladder. They got the corner office, the executive parking spot, the title that impresses people at parties. They have everything society told them to chase. And they're dying inside, one day at a time, wondering if this is really all there is.

Now let me show you the flip side, the other end of this equation. The teacher who discovered that her DNA-encoded purpose was teaching—not just any teaching, but specifically helping struggling kids learn to read—and she started offering online tutoring courses from her kitchen table. She makes a third of what she used to make in her corporate job. A third. Most people would call that failure. She's happier than she's been in twenty years because she's finally doing what's encoded in her genes. Or the lawyer who walked away from a six-figure salary to coach high school basketball. Everyone thought he was crazy. Took an eighty percent pay cut. Eighty percent. He has zero regrets because he's living his DNA-driven purpose every day.

What's the difference between these two groups? What separates the miserable millionaire from the fulfilled person working for a fraction of that income? Alignment. Pure, simple alignment. When what you do every day matches who you are at your genetic core, when your DNA-driven purpose and your daily work become the same thing, money stops being the point. It doesn't become irrelevant—you still need to pay bills, put food on the table, take care of your family. But it stops being the measuring stick for whether your life has meaning. You're finally living instead of just surviving.

What Actually Matters

The greatest things in life, the experiences and moments that actually matter when you look back on your years here, don't cost anything. I know that sounds like something you'd see on a bumper sticker or a motivational poster in an office break room. It sounds cliché. But stay with me because this is true in a way that most people never grasp, never fully understand until it's almost too late.

Your kid running to hug you when you get home from work, throwing their arms around you like you're the most important person in their universe. The deep, soul-level satisfaction you feel when you help someone who really needs it and you don't want anything in return. The feeling of creating something that matters, something that will outlast you, something that expresses what's been encoded in your DNA all along. The peace—the deep, unshakeable peace—that comes from knowing you're doing what you were born to do, living the purpose that's been written in your genes since before you took your first breath. None of this is for sale. No amount of money can buy these experiences. You can't walk into a store and purchase the feeling of living aligned with your DNA-driven purpose.

Think of it like this, and really let this image settle in your mind: Your DNA-driven purpose is like a seed. It's been inside you since before you were born, since before you had any say in the matter. It's sitting there, waiting. But here's what most people do with that seed—they spend their entire lives watering someone else's garden. They pour all their energy, all their time, all their talent into making someone else's vision grow while their own seed sits in the dark, never getting the light it needs, never breaking through the soil, never becoming what it was designed to become. Then one day they're sixty or seventy years old and they look around at this beautiful garden they helped create and they realize it's not theirs. It never was theirs. Their own seed is still sitting there in the dark, and now it might be too late to do anything about it.

But when you finally plant your own seed in the right conditions— when you give it the light and water and care it needs, when you stop spending all your energy on someone else's garden and start tending to your own—it grows into something only you could create.

Something that has your unique fingerprints all over it. Something that couldn't exist if you hadn't discovered and lived your DNA-driven purpose.

Jeff Bezos, with all his billions, can't buy the feeling of living aligned with his DNA-driven purpose any more than you can. Bill Gates can't purchase it. Elon Musk can't negotiate for it. The poorest person on earth has exactly the same access to purpose that the richest person has. It's written into them in exactly the same way it's written into billionaires. The only difference, the only thing that separates those who find it from those who don't, is whether you're willing to dig deep enough, look honestly enough, work hard enough to find it.

Purpose doesn't care about your resume, doesn't care how many degrees you have hanging on your wall. It doesn't care how many Instagram followers you've piled up or how impressive your LinkedIn profile looks. It only cares about one thing: whether you're willing to do the hard, uncomfortable work of figuring out who you actually are beneath all the layers of what you've been told to be, and then living like it.

Most people aren't willing to do that work. They'd rather have the comfortable lie than the uncomfortable truth. They'd rather keep chasing the next promotion, the bigger house, the nicer car, because at least that pursuit gives them something to do, something to focus on that doesn't require them to ask hard questions. It distracts them from the real question, the question that terrifies them if they're honest: What was I actually put here to do? What's encoded in my DNA that I've been ignoring?

That question scares people because once you ask it sincerely, once you really start looking for the answer, your entire life might have to change. The career you spent twenty years building might turn out to be wrong. The identity you've been showing the world might be fake.

The person you've been pretending to be might need to die so the real you can finally live. But here's what happens when you find the answer, when you discover your DNA-driven purpose and start living it: Everything shifts. The work that used to feel like drudgery becomes engaging. The relationships that used to drain you either transform or naturally fall away. The money you were desperately chasing becomes a byproduct of doing work that actually matters to you.

The Real Wealth

History gives us powerful, undeniable examples of people who had nothing by our culture's standards but everything by the standards that actually matter. Mother Teresa owned nothing. Not a car, not a house, not a savings account. She lived in the slums of Calcutta among the poorest people on earth, the people everyone else had forgotten about or given up on. By every measure our culture uses to determine success—income, assets, possessions, social status—she was a complete failure. Yet she radiated a contentment, a deep inner peace and joy, that millionaires and billionaires would trade their entire portfolios to feel for even a day.

What this example shows us, what it proves beyond any doubt: She had discovered her DNA-driven purpose. She knew exactly what she was born to do. She aligned her entire life—every single day, every decision, every action—around that purpose. The lack of material wealth became completely irrelevant because she was finally living the life encoded in her genes. She wasn't pretending to be someone she wasn't. She wasn't building someone else's dream. She was being exactly who God made her to be.

Viktor Frankl survived Nazi concentration camps, lived through experiences that would break most people permanently. He came out of that hell talking about meaning as the only thing that truly matters. Not comfort. Not safety. Not wealth. Not even survival itself. Meaning. Purpose. In the camps, he observed something remarkable:

The people who held onto their sense of purpose, who maintained connection to their DNA-encoded calling even in the worst conditions imaginable, survived situations that broke others who had lost their sense of meaning. Purpose, he learned through the harshest teacher possible, provides a kind of strength that no amount of comfort, no amount of wealth, no amount of security can match.

Here's the truth these examples reveal: Material wealth without purpose, without alignment with your DNA-driven calling, leads to emptiness and despair. No matter how much you accumulate, it's never enough. The hole inside never gets filled. But purpose without material wealth—purpose lived fully even in difficult circumstances—can create a life that overflows with richness, meaning, and satisfaction. The wealth that actually matters, the wealth that endures, can't be deposited in a bank account or displayed in a trophy case. It comes from the alignment between the purpose encoded in your DNA before you were born and the life you're actually living right now.

How Purpose Connects Us

Finding your DNA-driven purpose isn't something you do alone in a cave somewhere, isolated from everyone else. It can't be. Your DNA-encoded purpose connects to other people's purposes in ways you can't fully see or understand. They intersect. They support each other. They make each other stronger. Think of it like puzzle pieces—and really hold this image in your mind. Each piece is completely unique. No two are exactly the same. But each one is also designed, specifically designed, to fit with certain other pieces. Your purpose fits with specific other people's purposes. When you find yours and start living it, you naturally start connecting with people whose purposes complement yours.

When you discover what's written in your genes and start living it, when you stop pretending and start being real, something happens that you can't plan or manufacture. People notice. Not because you're trying to inspire them or because you're putting on some motivational show. They notice because you're being yourself for the first time in your life and being real is magnetic. Your willingness to live your DNA-driven purpose gives other people permission to examine their own lives, to ask whether they might be living outside their genetic design too.

This is how real change spreads through families, communities, entire cultures. Not through programs or campaigns or viral videos. Through the simple, powerful act of one person discovering their DNA-driven purpose and having the courage to live it. One person finds theirs and lives it authentically. Three people around them start asking questions about their own lives, wondering if they too might be walking the wrong path. One of those three makes a change, takes a risk, steps into their own purpose. Two people watch that person and get brave enough to do the same. The numbers grow and multiply, not because anyone's preaching or pushing, but because people living their purpose naturally inspire others to find theirs.

Your DNA-encoded purpose touches your family first, starts there at home. When you come home from work energized instead of drained, when your eyes light up talking about what you did today instead of complaining about what you have to endure, your kids see it. They learn something crucial: that adults don't have to be miserable, that work doesn't have to be something you suffer through, that there's another way to live. Your spouse sees you actually alive instead of just going through the motions, and something shifts in your relationship. The whole temperature, the whole feel of your home changes when even one person starts living their DNA-driven purpose.

Then it spreads beyond what you can directly see or measure. The work you do while living your DNA-driven purpose creates value that extends outward in ways you'll never fully know about. The person you mentor this year goes on to mentor three others next year. The business you build around your purpose employs ten people who use that income to fund their kids' college education. The art you create touches someone you'll never meet and changes their entire path. This is how purpose works when it's aligned with your DNA. It's always bigger than you. Always connected. Always part of something larger than what you can see from your limited perspective.

The Gift You've Been Given

God didn't randomly assign your DNA like rolling dice. He didn't accidentally give you the specific combination of abilities, passions, and perspectives you have. He put them into you deliberately, intentionally, before you were born, before you had any say in the matter. That wasn't an accident or a cosmic coincidence. You were made for something particular, something specific, something that only you can do in exactly the way you can do it because of how your DNA is wired.

This is the gift I'm talking about. Not that your life will be easy if you find your purpose—it probably won't be. Not that you'll get rich—you might or you might not, and that's not really the point anyway. The gift is that you get to live aligned with who you actually are instead of spending your entire life pretending to be someone you're not. You get to experience the deep, soul-level satisfaction of doing what you were made to do. You get to feel your DNA-driven purpose and your daily existence become the same thing instead of being split in two, torn between who you are and what you do.

Most people never open this gift. They walk right past it their entire lives. They're too distracted by shinier packages, more attractive options—the promise of wealth, the allure of status, the comfort of security, the approval of others. They spend forty, fifty, sixty years reaching for things that were never meant to fulfill them, pouring all their energy into pursuits that can't possibly satisfy what's missing, ignoring the one thing that would actually make them feel complete.

Opening this gift requires real work, often painful work. You have to be willing to peel back layers and layers of what other people told you to be. Your parents' dreams for you. Your spouse's expectations. Your culture's definitions of success. Your own assumptions about what your life is supposed to look like. You have to challenge beliefs you've held since you were five years old, beliefs that feel like facts because you've never questioned them. You have to look at things everyone around you treats as obvious truth and ask, "But is it true for me? Does this align with what's encoded in my DNA?" You have to face fears about what you'll lose if you step into your real purpose—the approval of people you care about, the security of a steady paycheck, the comfortable identity you've built over decades. You have to admit to yourself, and maybe to others, that you've been pretending, that the life you've built might not actually be yours.

This is why so few people do it. This is why ninety-eight and a half percent of people live their entire lives disconnected from their DNA-driven purpose. Not because the gift isn't available—it's sitting right there, has been there all along. But because unwrapping it, opening it, receiving what's inside is hard. It's uncomfortable. It requires change. But here's what I know from living both ways, from experiencing life disconnected from my purpose and then finding it: Living outside your DNA-encoded purpose is harder. Much harder. The slow, grinding death of working a job that kills a little piece of your soul every single day. The quiet, desperate feeling of pretending to be someone you're not for so long that you can barely remember who you actually are underneath the mask. The accumulating regret that builds up year after year as you watch your one irreplaceable life slip away unlived, knowing you're not doing what you were born to do. That's the real hard. That's the unbearable hard.

Finding your DNA-driven purpose is hard too. I'm not going to lie to you and say it's easy. But it's the kind of hard that leads somewhere meaningful. The kind of hard that builds something that lasts. The kind of hard that, when you're eighty years old and looking back on your life, makes you smile with satisfaction instead of weep with regret. The kind of hard that lets you die knowing you actually lived.

Before you turn this page, I need you to do one thing. It takes thirty seconds.

Grab whatever's closest — a pen, your phone, the margin of this page. Write down the one thing you'd do with your life if money and approval vanished tomorrow. Don't edit it. Don't make it sound smart. Don't worry about whether it's realistic.

Just write the first thing that comes up.

That's your DNA talking. That's Chapter 2.

CHAPTER 2: THE CRUCIBLE OF CLARITY – UNEARTHING THE "WHY"

Life, in its relentless rhythm, in its day-after-day predictability, often lulls us into a state of lazy comfort where we stop seeing miracles as miracles. You breathe without thinking about it, without marveling at the complex biological process that keeps you alive second after second. Your heart beats on its own, pumping blood through thousands of miles of vessels, and you never stop to appreciate that it's been doing this job perfectly without your conscious control since before you were born. You wake up every morning and your body just works, your mind processes thoughts, your senses take in the world, and it all seems so normal, so ordinary, so guaranteed that we forget how fragile this whole thing actually is. We stop feeling grateful for the everyday miracle of being alive. We just assume this is how life is, how it will always be, that we have unlimited time to figure out what we're supposed to be doing here.

Then something happens that rips the curtain down, that shatters the illusion of permanence, that forces you to see how thin the line is between being here and being gone.

The Day Everything Changed

For me, it was twelve minutes of absolute nothing. No heartbeat. No breath. No consciousness. No me. Three blood clots—pulmonary embolisms, the doctors called them—decided to kill me on what had been a perfectly ordinary Tuesday afternoon. I wasn't old. I wasn't sick. I had no warning, no symptoms, no reason to think this particular Tuesday would be any different from the thousands of other Tuesdays I'd lived through. But these clots had different plans. They decided I was done.

My family stood around me, their faces distorted with fear and grief, crying because they thought they were watching me leave this world. And for twelve minutes, I did leave. Twelve full minutes. That's a long time to be dead. I don't know where I went. I can't explain what happened during that time. I just know that I was gone, completely gone, and then somehow I came back.

In that space between here and gone, in those moments when I was standing at the edge of existence, everything got clear with a speed and intensity that's hard to describe. All the arguments I'd been holding onto, all the grudges I'd been nursing, all the petty resentments I'd been feeding for months or years—they revealed themselves as completely, utterly meaningless. The drama I'd let myself get tangled up in, the conflicts that had seemed so important just hours before, the worries about what people thought of me—all of it burned away like fog in sunlight. When you're staring at the actual edge of existence, when you're about to cross over into whatever comes next, the small stuff doesn't just seem small. It vanishes. What's left is what actually matters, stripped of all the noise and distraction.

God brought me back. I don't say that lightly, and I'm not trying to convince you of anything or prove anything about theology. I'm just telling you what I know to be true in the deepest part of me: I was gone for twelve minutes, and then I wasn't. Something, someone, brought me back. And coming back after being gone that long, after crossing that line, meant something. It had to mean something. I had work left to do, some specific purpose that couldn't be accomplished if I stayed gone. Otherwise, why bring me back? Why not let me stay wherever I was?

The Questions That Wouldn't Let Go

I started praying differently after that experience. These weren't comfortable prayers offered out of habit or obligation, the kind of prayers you say because it's what you're supposed to do. These were desperate prayers, raw and urgent and borderline demanding. The kind of prayers where you're not asking politely, where you're begging for answers because not knowing feels unbearable. I needed to understand why I was still breathing. What purpose justified pulling me back from wherever I'd been. What God wanted from me that He couldn't get from someone else, some other person who hadn't just spent twelve minutes dead on a hot concrete parking lot.

The answers didn't come in a dramatic moment. There was no voice from heaven, no burning bush, no angel appearing with a scroll. The answers came in pieces, slowly, like a puzzle being assembled one fragment at a time over weeks and months. They came through conversations that happened at exactly the right moment with exactly the right person. Through people who showed up out of nowhere—people I hadn't spoken to in years, people I'd just met, complete strangers—carrying exactly what I needed to hear in that moment. Through doors that opened when I wasn't even looking for them and slammed shut decisively when I tried to push too hard in the wrong direction.

God started rearranging my life in ways I could never have arranged myself. People who had been part of my world for years, people I'd thought would be there forever, quietly faded out. There were no dramatic fights or ugly confrontations. Our paths just diverged naturally as our DNA-driven purposes pulled us in different directions. It wasn't that they were bad people or that I was. We just weren't meant to walk the same road anymore. Meanwhile, new people appeared seemingly out of nowhere. A mentor at a conference I almost decided not to attend. An old friend who called at 2 a.m. because they couldn't sleep and neither could I, and in that late-night conversation, something clicked into place.

I didn't plan any of this. I couldn't have planned it if I tried. God was connecting dots I couldn't see yet, arranging circumstances in ways that only made sense in retrospect. He was clearing away the clutter, removing what didn't belong, and building the foundation for what was coming next. All I had to do—and this was harder than it sounds—was pay attention. Notice what was happening. Follow where He was leading instead of trying to force my own agenda.

The Vision Takes Shape

The vision for what I was supposed to do, what all this was leading toward, started coming into focus gradually. Not all at once in one dramatic revelation—I'm still discovering new layers of it even now. But the core, the essential center of it, became clear enough that I couldn't ignore it or pretend I didn't see it: I was here to help people discover the purpose encoded in their DNA. To show them that the life they're currently living, the one they've spent decades building, might not be the life they were actually born to live. To give them the tools and framework to dig through all the layers of conditioning and expectation until they hit the bedrock of who they really are.

This is when the ninety-eight and a half percent number started haunting me, keeping me up at night, refusing to let me rest. If only one or two people out of every hundred are actually living in alignment with their DNA-driven purpose, that means billions— literally billions—of people are walking around disconnected from what they were born to do. Billions of human lives being spent, used up, consumed on purposes and paths that were never theirs to begin with. Billions of unique contributions, specific gifts that only they could make, dying with them because they never discovered what was encoded in their DNA.

Think about that number. Really let it sink in. Look around next time you're in a crowded restaurant or a shopping mall or walking down a busy street. Look at all those faces, all those people going about their lives. Ninety-eight out of every hundred of them are not living the life written into their genes. They're living the life their parents designed for them before they were old enough to know better. The life their culture told them they should want. The life that seemed practical or safe or like the path of least resistance. They're spending forty, fifty, sixty years building someone else's dream, pursuing someone else's definition of success, becoming someone they were never meant to be.

And here's the thing that breaks my heart: This isn't their fault. Nobody wakes up one day and decides to live disconnected from their DNA-driven purpose. Nobody chooses this deliberately. We're never taught how to find our purpose. Think about your education. School taught you algebra that you've never used once as an adult. It taught you to memorize dates and facts that have zero relevance to your actual life. But discovering who you actually are? Finding what's encoded in your DNA? Learning to recognize the difference between your authentic self and the person you've been told to be? That's not in any curriculum. Your parents probably tried their best, but most of them never found their own DNA-driven purpose, so how could they possibly guide you to yours? They were just repeating the patterns that were handed down to them. And society? Society doesn't want you to discover your unique purpose. It wants you to be productive, to consume, to buy things. Your DNA-encoded calling is irrelevant to the economy unless it happens to align with what makes money.

So people stumble through life trying on different identities like they're shopping for clothes. This career for a few years. That relationship. This city, that apartment. This friend group. Always searching for something they can't quite name. Always feeling like something essential is missing but never quite putting their finger on what it is. The lucky ones keep searching. The unlucky ones give up, decide the emptiness is just part of being an adult, and resign themselves to quiet desperation for the next forty years.

When Who You Are and What You Do Become One
There's a level of existence that most people never reach, never even know exists. Most people live their entire lives at what I call survival level. They're working to pay the bills, trying to make it through the week without disaster, hoping to have a little bit left over for

themselves after all the obligations are met. The goal is just to keep the lights on and food on the table. There's no energy or time left for bigger questions about meaning or purpose. Survival is all they can manage.

Some people move beyond survival to what looks like success. They get the nice house in the good neighborhood. The solid income that covers more than just basics. The respect of their peers. They've climbed the ladder, checked off the boxes society says to check off, and from the outside, it looks like winning. It looks like they've figured it out. But then there's this moment—maybe it comes at forty, maybe at fifty or sixty—where they wake up and realize that success isn't the same as fulfillment. They have everything they were supposed to want, and they feel empty anyway. The success they spent decades chasing doesn't actually satisfy what's missing inside them.

Then there's what I call the Purpose Level. This is the level where ninety-eight and a half percent of people never arrive. This is where who you are and what you do finally stop being two different things pulling you in opposite directions. Where your DNA-driven purpose and your daily life become so perfectly aligned that the distinction between "work" and "life" stops making sense. Where you're doing what you were made to do, what's encoded in your genes, so work doesn't feel like work anymore. It feels like living.

At this level, time starts behaving strangely. You lose hours—whole afternoons vanish—in work that energizes you instead of draining you. You look up and realize the sun has set and you forgot to eat lunch and you're not tired, you're exhilarated. Challenges that would crush someone living outside their purpose feel like interesting problems you were specifically designed to solve. Money still matters—you still need to pay bills, take care of your family—but it stops being the measuring stick for whether your life has meaning.

You'd do this work for free if you had to because it's an expression of who you are, not just a way to earn income.

This is where the one percent lives. Not the financial one percent—though some of them are wealthy and some aren't, because that's not actually the point. I'm talking about the purpose one percent. The people who figured out what's written in their DNA and had the courage to build their entire lives around it, even when everyone told them they were crazy for walking away from security or status or the path that was supposed to make sense.

They're not all rich. Some are wealthy. Many aren't. The teacher making forty thousand dollars a year who lights up every single student she works with because teaching is what's encoded in her DNA and she knows it. The carpenter who creates furniture so beautiful people keep it for generations because working with his hands to create something that lasts is his DNA-driven purpose. The nurse who makes patients feel truly seen and cared for in their most vulnerable moments because that's what she was born to do. The entrepreneur who built a business around solving a problem she's genuinely passionate about, not because it was the most profitable option but because it's what her DNA was calling her toward.

Money often follows purpose—that's a pattern you see again and again. But it's never the point. The point is alignment. The point is living like you actually mean it instead of just going through the motions. The point is getting to the end of your life and being able to look back knowing you spent your years being exactly who you were made to be instead of someone else's idea of who you should have been.

Finding Your "Why"

Finding your DNA-driven purpose, discovering your "why," isn't some mysterious process that requires years of meditation on a mountaintop or thousands of dollars spent on therapy and retreats.

There are specific, practical questions you can ask yourself. Clear patterns you can learn to identify. Concrete signs pointing you toward what's encoded in your genes, waiting to be discovered and lived.

Start by paying attention to energy—not just whether you feel tired or awake, but what activities make time completely disappear. I'm not talking about passive escape, about scrolling social media for three hours or binge-watching an entire series. I'm talking about active engagement where you're fully present, fully involved, and you look up suddenly realizing that hours have vanished and you have no idea where they went. That's your DNA recognizing work it was designed to do. That flow state, that complete absorption, is a clue your genes are trying to give you about your purpose.

Look at what makes you genuinely angry, not just annoyed or frustrated. What problems in the world make your blood boil? What injustices can you not stop thinking about? What situations make you want to scream "Why isn't anyone doing something about this?" That anger isn't random. It's not just a personality flaw you need to manage. It's fuel. It's your DNA pointing you toward a problem you were specifically built to help solve. The things that make you angry often reveal what you're meant to fix.

Notice what you're naturally good at, what skills come easily to you while other people struggle. The way you see solutions that others miss. The patterns you recognize that are invisible to everyone else. The abilities that feel so natural you don't even think of them as special. Your DNA came pre-loaded with specific gifts, particular strengths that are unique to your genetic code. Most people overlook these because they seem too easy, too natural. But that ease is a sign, not something to dismiss.

Pay attention to what people consistently ask you for help with. What advice do friends seek from you? What problems do colleagues bring to you? What role do you naturally fill in groups? Other people often see your DNA-driven purpose more clearly than you do because they're watching from the outside. They recognize your unique contribution, the thing you offer that nobody else does quite the same way, even when you don't see it yourself because it's just how you naturally operate.

This process of discovery isn't a weekend workshop. It's not something you knock out in an afternoon. It's excavation work—real, sustained digging through layers and layers of piled up conditioning. You're removing what your parents told you to want before you were old enough to know what you actually wanted. Clearing away what seemed practical when you were choosing a college major or taking that first job. Stripping off what looked impressive to the people whose approval you craved. Peeling back what you thought you should be. You're digging and digging until you finally hit bedrock— the solid, unshakeable foundation of who you actually are beneath everything that's been piled on top.

Some people hit that bedrock relatively quickly. Most don't. Most have to chip away at these layers for months, sometimes years, removing one false belief at a time, questioning one assumption after another. But every piece they remove, every layer they strip away, reveals a little bit more of the DNA-driven purpose that's been sitting there all along, waiting to be uncovered and lived.

Your "Why" Powers Your "What"

You can do almost anything. This is both the blessing and the curse of being human. We're remarkably adaptable creatures. We can force ourselves into careers we secretly hate. We can maintain that forced performance for decades, showing up day after day to do work that slowly kills something inside us. We can smile through it. We can even convince ourselves, at least on the surface, that it's fine, that this is just what being an adult means, that everyone feels this way.

But imagine—really let yourself imagine—what happens when your "what" finally aligns with your "why." When the work you do every day connects directly to the purpose encoded in your DNA. When you stop forcing yourself to be someone you're not and start being yourself at full volume, with no apologies and no pretense. Everything about how you experience life shifts in ways that are hard to explain to someone who hasn't felt it.

The energy is completely different. You're not dragging yourself out of bed every Monday morning, hitting the snooze button three times, dreading the week ahead. You wake up naturally with ideas already forming, problems you're excited to solve, work you genuinely want to do. Challenges stop feeling like obstacles blocking your path. They become interesting problems you were specifically designed to figure out. Setbacks don't destroy you or send you spiraling into despair. They redirect you, show you where you need to adjust your approach, reveal what's not aligned with your DNA-driven purpose.

This is why purpose matters more than raw talent. Talent without purpose burns out. The talented person who doesn't know their "why" hits a wall eventually. They run out of motivation. They start wondering what the point is. They achieve success that feels empty. But purpose combined with even modest talent? That person will outlast, outwork, out-persist the talented person every single time. Because they know their "why." They understand what their DNA is calling them to do. That knowledge, that alignment, fuels everything. It gets them through the hard times when talent alone would give up.

Most people spend their entire working lives—forty years, fifty years, their entire adult existence—laboring on someone else's "what," powered by someone else's "why." They're building someone else's vision. Making someone else's dream come true. Living someone else's version of success. No wonder they come home exhausted every night. No wonder they need the weekends just to recover enough energy to face another week. They're living a borrowed life, and the weight of that inauthenticity is crushing even when they can't name what's wrong.

Finding your "why"—discovering and embracing your DNA-driven purpose—changes everything, transforms your entire experience of being alive. Suddenly the career that actually fits you becomes obvious. The relationships that genuinely matter start making sense. The contribution that's uniquely yours, that only you can make in exactly this way, reveals itself. The life you were actually meant to live, the one encoded in your genes since before you were born, comes into sharp focus. And once you see it, you can't unsee it. Once you know what your DNA-driven purpose is, living any other way becomes impossible to tolerate.

This is what I found lying on that cold ER table with my family crying around me. This is what twelve minutes of being dead taught me about actually living. This is why God brought me back instead of letting me stay wherever I was during those twelve minutes. Not so I could keep doing what I'd been doing before, keep living the way I'd been living. But so I could discover my own DNA-encoded purpose and then spend whatever time I have left helping other people discover theirs.

The question isn't whether you have a DNA-driven purpose. You absolutely do. Every single person does. Everyone has something specific encoded in their genes, some unique contribution they're designed to make. The question is whether you'll do the hard work required to find it. Whether you'll dig deep enough through all the layers of conditioning and expectation. Whether you'll be brave enough to live it once you finally discover what it is, even if living it means disappointing people or changing everything about your current life.

Most people won't do that work. They'll stay comfortable in the ninety-eight point five percent. They'll keep chasing what they've been told to chase. They'll keep building someone else's dream. They'll keep pretending to be someone they're not. And they'll die one day having never discovered, never lived, the purpose that was encoded in their DNA all along.

But some people will do the work. Some will read these words and feel something shift inside them, some recognition that what I'm describing is real and true and applies to them. Some will start asking the hard questions. Some will begin the excavation, start digging through all those layers. Some will find what's been sitting there in their DNA since before they were born, waiting to be discovered and activated and lived. Some will have the courage to step into that purpose even when it's scary, even when it costs them something, even when other people don't understand.

Those are the ones who change everything. Not just for themselves, but for everyone around them. Those are the ones who shift from the ninety-eight point five percent into the one point five percent. Those are the ones who finally live. And you have everything they have.

Now let me ask you something directly.

You know your Why. You've felt it. Maybe you've been carrying it for years and haven't had the permission to say it out loud.

Say it. Right now. Out loud or in writing — doesn't matter. One sentence: "The reason I am here is…"

Don't finish the sentence with your job title. Don't finish it with what you've always been told to want.

Finish it with what you know.

We build on that sentence in Chapter 3.

CHAPTER 3: THE PURPOSE REVEALED — A PROCESS OF UNVEILING AND POWER

Let me tell you something that changed my entire life. I believe—with staggering, almost unbelievable certainty—it can change yours too.

There comes a moment when the fog lifts. Not a little. Not partway. I mean the kind of clearing where you finally see the road ahead. Every step you took in the dark suddenly makes sense. Every bruise has a reason. Every delay has a purpose.

Divine help—prayers answered, paths lit up by a hand steadier than your own—is not some abstract idea to me. It is lived experience. It is the air I breathe.

Picture the shift that happens when uncertainty doesn't just fade—it gets ripped away. The divine hand guides your steps with clear, undeniable direction. That's what happened to me.

My unanswered prayers—the silence that made me wonder if anyone was listening—gave way to a flood of purpose. Confusion turned into bone-deep conviction. The scattered, broken pieces of my life came together into something that finally made sense.

This wasn't a motivational poster moment. It wasn't a feel-good flash that faded by Tuesday. This shift rebuilt my life from the inside out. My relationships changed. My goals changed. My understanding of what it means to be alive—changed.

If you're reading this and you're still lost in that fog—still asking "Why am I here?" at three in the morning—stay with me. I've been exactly where you are. I know the way through.

Clearing the Path

The path was buried at first. Not just cloudy—buried under the clutter and chaos of a life without direction. Noise from every angle. Distractions pulling me sideways. I couldn't tell what mattered from what was just loud.

It was a season of hard, even painful self-reflection. Think of it like cleaning out a garage that hasn't been touched in twenty years. You have to pull everything out. You have to look at it under good light. Some of it you keep. Most of it, you realize, was just taking up space.

I had to clear out the negativity and self-doubt piled up over years of living cut off from my DNA-driven purpose. Years where I was running hard but running in circles. Sweating but never arriving.

Seeing the things blocking me from God's blessings was the first humbling step. And humbling doesn't cover it. It was sobering the way truth always is—not cruel, but relentless.

Here's what hit me: our own limits—the stories we've told ourselves so many times they feel like facts—become walls. They block the very blessings we claim to want. We build the prison, then wonder why we're stuck.

Street Translation: You can't receive what you're not ready to hold. It's like trying to catch a football with both hands full of groceries. Something has to go down before something new can come in.

You've been praying for a breakthrough. Asking God for the next level. But your hands are full of things from the last season. Old grudges. Old habits. Old versions of yourself you keep because they're familiar.

The blessing is trying to reach you. There's just no room for it to land. In your real life, this looks like admitting the relationship you keep defending is the thing draining you. Or the job you cling to for safety is the cage keeping you from your calling.

Clearing obstacles isn't a one-time event. It's not a Saturday clean-up you check off a list. It's a daily discipline. It demands watchfulness and a level of commitment most people won't sustain.

Each day brings new distractions and new chances to drift off course. The world doesn't stop throwing noise at you just because you decided to listen for something quieter. You have to keep choosing. Every single day.

Think of it like tuning a guitar. You don't tune it once and play forever. Temperature changes. Strings stretch. You have to keep checking and adjusting. Same with your purpose.

Among the sneakiest, most deep-rooted obstacles are the limiting beliefs we carry about ourselves. I know them well. I carried them for years—heavy, invisible, sewn into every decision I made.

These beliefs usually form in childhood or through painful experiences. They become self-fulfilling predictions. They shrink your vision. They cap your potential in ways you don't even see. You don't notice the cage when you were born inside it.

Naming and fighting these beliefs is essential. Absolutely critical. Without that fight, there's no room—no breathable space—for the purpose written in your DNA to surface.

Outside obstacles hit just as hard. Sometimes harder, because they wear friendly faces.

Draining relationships that suck your energy drop by drop until you wake up empty. Work places that poison your spirit slowly—like carbon monoxide, invisible and quiet but deadly over time.

Money pressure that forces you to compromise until you forget what you were aiming for. Social expectations that demand you walk a path that isn't yours—a path that looks fine from outside but feels like slow suffocation from within.

We can't always change our circumstances overnight. Anyone who says otherwise is selling something. But we can change how we respond. We can choose where we put our energy. We can choose whose voice gets a vote in our future.

I remember a season when every outside force seemed stacked against me. Money tight. Relationships strained. Doors closing faster than I could knock. I felt like a boxer in the eighth round with nothing left. But here's what I learned in that ring: it's not about how hard you get hit. It's about whether you keep your feet under you. You clear the path one step at a time. Not by removing every obstacle at once. That's a fantasy. You clear it by refusing to quit on the one step right in front of you.

Think of it like weeding a garden. You don't pull every weed in one afternoon. You pull what you can see today. Tomorrow, new ones will show up. That's fine. You pull those too. The point isn't a perfect garden. The point is that you keep tending the soil so the right things have room to grow.

The Transformative Mindset Shift

The trigger for change was a deep, ground-level mindset shift. Not a tweak. A demolition. The old framework came down and something new rose on cleared ground.

It wasn't a goosebump sermon. It wasn't a highlighted quote that felt powerful for fifteen minutes. It was a total rewiring of how I saw myself and what I expected from the horizon.

My focus sharpened to a razor's edge. The passion lit up—not a spark but a furnace. A relentless, almost unstoppable drive pushed me forward with a force I'd never felt.

This shift wasn't something I did alone in a quiet room. It was a team effort with God. He brought people into my life who became pillars, encouragers, and partners in the chase for DNA-driven purpose.

I've been in the place where the shift hasn't happened yet. Reading the books. Going to the conferences. Saying the right words. Still stuck. I know that frustration like I know my own face.

Here's what I learned: the shift isn't something you build. It's something you position yourself to receive. It's like planting a garden—you prepare the soil, you plant the seed, you water it. But you don't make it grow. That part comes from somewhere else.

When the shift comes, it changes everything. Things that scared you become small. People who shook you become peers. Goals that seemed crazy become certain. Not because you changed overnight. Because how you see changed—and when how you see changes, what you can do changes with it.

This shift had several connected parts, like tumblers in a lock. Each one needed. None enough alone.

From scarcity to plenty: seeing that there's more than enough to go around. The world is not a pie where your slice means less for me.

From fear to faith: trusting a divine plan instead of freezing up. Believing the purpose in your DNA will show up on time—even when your patience runs thin.

From comparison to calling: letting go of the need to measure your path against someone else's highlight reel. Focusing on the one purpose no one else can fill because no one else is you.

From comfort to growth: treating discomfort like a training partner, not an enemy. Challenges aren't walls. They're weight rooms. They build what comfort never could.

From being alone to being together: seeing that purpose grows in connection. Our DNA-driven purposes cross paths and multiply when we link up.

Street Translation: You have to change the station before you can change your life. Most of us play the same loop—fear, doubt, comparison, repeat—and wonder why everything feels stale.

Shifting your mind isn't about "thinking positive." It's about thinking true. It's telling yourself: "I'm not stuck because I lack talent. I'm stuck because I've been pointing my talent the wrong way."

In your daily life, this shows up when you stop scrolling someone else's wins and start building your own. It shows up when you catch yourself saying "I could never" and you correct it—not with blind hope, but with honest truth: "I haven't tried yet."

This change didn't show up in a flash. No angels. No soundtrack. It was built brick by brick through daily habits.

Gratitude when nothing felt worth thanking God for. Seeing the future in my mind when reality looked nothing like it. Speaking truth over myself when it felt like arguing with my own reflection.

I had to choose what I watched, what I talked about, and what thoughts I let plant roots in my mind. Every input was either feeding my purpose or starving it. There was no middle ground.

Let me be real with you about what this looked like day to day. It wasn't glamorous. Some mornings I sat in my car before work and spoke truth out loud to myself because my own thoughts were lying to me. Some nights I turned off the TV because every show was reinforcing a story I needed to stop believing. I deleted phone numbers. I left group chats. I started guarding my mind the way you'd guard a house with your children inside—because what gets in will shape what grows.

Think of your mind like a kitchen. If you stock the fridge with junk, you'll eat junk—not because you're weak, but because that's what's there. Stock it with real food and your choices change without willpower. Same with your inputs. Fill your mind with fear-based media, comparison loops, and gossip? That's what your thoughts will cook with. Fill it with truth, vision, and people who challenge you to grow? Different meal entirely.

Divine Connections

These were not accidents. Not lucky breaks. They were divinely set-up meetings—planned by a God who sees the whole picture when we can barely see the next step.

God started rearranging my life in ways I never could have planned. People who had drained me for years—not bad people, just wrong-season people—faded out. No fight. No drama. Just a quiet drifting apart that felt natural, like a tide pulling back.

Meanwhile, new people appeared out of nowhere. A mentor at a conference I almost skipped because I was tired. An old friend who called at two in the morning because neither of us could sleep. That one call changed both our paths.

A stranger at a coffee shop said one sentence that opened a door in my mind I didn't know was shut. I can still hear the espresso machine in the background. I can still feel the weight of that moment when everything inside me shifted.

These connections came in forms I never predicted. Mentors who'd walked hard roads and could guide from real experience. Peers on parallel paths who got it without me having to explain. Younger voices that brought fresh sight and reminded me that this mission is bigger than my lifetime.

Even unlikely allies showed up at make-or-break moments with exactly what was needed.

What made these connections so powerful was how they fit together. Like a sports team where each player covers the other's blind spot. Each person brought something no one else had—specific skills, views, resources, or relationships that filled gaps I hadn't noticed.

Together, our results were staggering, almost unbelievable compared to what any of us could have done solo. Individual ability multiplied when linked to shared, DNA-driven purpose.

These meetings often came right when needed. Sometimes before I even knew the need existed. A conference handshake led to a key partnership months later. A random introduction opened doors that seemed welded shut.

An old contact popped back up with exactly the skill set the next phase required. As if summoned by the purpose itself.

I've learned that God builds teams the way a master chef builds a recipe. Each ingredient matters. Leave one out and the dish falls flat. Add the wrong one and it ruins the whole thing. But when every piece lands in the right place at the right time? The result is something none of the parts could have been alone.

If you're waiting for connections and they haven't come yet, let me tell you what I wish someone had told me: you're not being forgotten. You're being prepared. And so are they. The timing isn't late. It's loading.

Street Translation: God is a master connector, and His timing is surgical. The right person shows up right when you need them. But only if you're awake enough to notice.

That mentor might not look like what you expected. That door might come wrapped in something you'd normally skip. In your real life, this means saying yes to the event you almost blew off. Returning the call you almost ignored. Staying open to the person who doesn't fit your usual circle but carries exactly what your next season needs.

The Birth of "Step Into Success"

Out of this life-changing season came the "Step Into Success" program. It wasn't just a concept. Not an idea on a napkin. It was a calling—a divine order to lift up people who'd been pushed aside by the world's standard playbook for success.

The program was born from a staggering, almost unbelievable truth: 98.5% of people live their whole lives cut off from their DNA-driven purpose. They never find what makes them one-of-a-kind. They never switch on the blueprint for meaning that lives inside them.

Let that number settle in your chest. In a room of two hundred, only three have found and are living their purpose. The rest are surviving. Working. Going through motions. But not truly living.

The vision didn't arrive as a finished plan. It came like a seed. It opened slowly through prayer that sometimes felt like begging. Through reflection that felt like wrestling. Through God's voice arriving in pieces I had to put together with faith.

Early ideas led to tests. Tests led to fine-tuning. Fine-tuning led to a clear system for helping people reach what's been coded in their DNA all along—waiting, patient, ready.

One thing became impossible to deny: the program had to serve the whole person. Not just head knowledge, which is where most programs stop. It needed heart healing. Spiritual grounding. And hands-on tools that turn "I see it" into "I'm living it."

The program sits on three pillars. They move people from confusion to clarity. From borrowed lives to DNA-driven purpose. These aren't ideas floating in the clouds. They're proven steps that work.

Part One: Discover — Digging Out the Real You

This first phase is digging work. I use that word on purpose because it's not gentle and it's not quick.

We dig through layers of what other people told you to be. What your parents expected. What your culture rewards. What seemed safe or impressive enough to justify at family dinners.

We chip through decades of buildup. Think of scraping old paint off a wall—layer after layer. Until we hit the original surface: who you actually are under all the acting.

This means facing questions you've been dodging. Maybe your whole life. What gives you energy versus what drains you? What makes you lose track of time? What problems make you angry enough to actually want to solve them—not just complain, but fix?

These aren't casual questions. They're signals. Flashing arrows pointing toward your DNA-coded purpose.

We start with thorough tests. They help people name their natural talents, core values, personality patterns, and emotional wiring. The specific setup of gifts baked into their DNA.

These tests act like mirrors. Not the kind you glance at rushing out the door. The kind where you stand under full light and see what's really there. Parts of yourself you've overlooked or pushed aside for years.

They give you words for your strengths without false humility. Words for your weak spots without shame. Names for what drives you and what warns you.

But discovery goes beyond tests. People get into hands-on experiences. They try new skills. They test different roles. They try on different ways of showing up the way you'd try on shoes—except these fit your soul.

These tries often shock people. Talents that sat dormant for decades wake up like seeds after rain. Passions buried under "responsible" choices surface. Connections between unrelated interests suddenly reveal the brilliant design of their DNA-driven purpose.

Most important: this phase makes room for deep listening. Listening to your inner voice—the one drowned out by noise for so long it might feel foreign. Listening to trusted people who see what you can't see in yourself. And listening to God's gentle nudges—the ones that come as whispers, not thunder.

It's in that sacred quiet that people first hear what their DNA has been saying all along.

Part Two: Define — Choosing Your One Path

Once discovery reveals the buried map of your DNA-coded gifts, the next step demands a hard choice. Often an agonizing one. You have to decide which path is truly yours.

Not three paths. Not "keeping options open"—which sounds wise but is really fear wearing a nice outfit. One clear direction written in your genetic code.

This phase turns raw insight into solid vision. It's about finding your unique strengths and building your entire life—not just your career, your whole life—around expressing them.

Think of it like a quarterback calling a play. He doesn't run three routes at once. He reads the field, picks the open lane, and commits. That's what Define is.

We help people answer questions most dodge their entire lives. What am I uniquely built to give? What problems was I born to solve? What would success look like measured by my real self?

This phase uses creative vision exercises. People imagine their ideal future in vivid detail. Not the future they think they should want. The one that makes their pulse quicken and their eyes fill with something between tears and fire.

They draft personal mission statements. They set goals bold enough to demand growth but clear enough to start today. They build a roadmap their DNA can actually follow.

Define also means setting hard boundaries. Getting brutally clear about what doesn't fit your DNA-driven purpose so you stop wasting time on it.

People learn to say no to good things that pull focus from the right thing. That's one of the hardest lessons: good is the enemy of great. They learn the gap between what they can do and what they were born to do. And they choose the born-to. Even when the can-do pays better.

Part Three: Develop — Building the Skills to Live It

The final phase is where vision crashes into real life. And real life doesn't flinch.

Knowing your DNA-driven purpose means nothing—absolutely nothing—if you don't have the skills to live it. This is where you close the gap between who you are now and who you need to become.

Think of a mechanic who knows what's wrong with the engine but doesn't have the wrench. Knowing isn't fixing. This phase puts the tools in your hands.

This is where sweat meets the dream. Where your Phase Two vision gets tested by alarm clocks, bills, setbacks, and the Monday morning question: "Do I still mean it?"

It starts with an honest look at where you are. No sugar-coating. Where's the gap between your present and your purpose? What skills do you need? What credentials? What relationships? What resources?

People build personal plans—some formal schooling, some hands-on practice, some trial and error that builds the kind of wisdom no classroom gives.

This phase stresses steady, inch-by-inch progress. Not dramatic overnight makeovers that look good online but collapse at the first real test. Break big goals into steps small enough to take today. Celebrate progress. Don't wait for perfection.

It also means building the right support systems. Daily habits that feed your purpose instead of fighting it. Routines that guard time for what matters most. Partners who tell you hard truths when you need them. Groups of like-minded people who cheer you on when the tank is empty.

Regular check-ins on what's working and what's not. Honest adjustments based on real results. Renewed commitment when the road ahead goes dark.

I compare this phase to training for a marathon. You don't run twenty-six miles on day one. You run one. Then two. Then five. Some days your legs ache and your mind says quit. You run anyway—not because you're special, but because you decided. Purpose works the same way. The decision to keep going on a hard Tuesday matters more than the excitement you felt on the first day.

I've seen people quit six inches from their breakthrough. Not because they lacked talent. Because they lacked support. That's why this phase isn't optional. It's the gap between a dream stuck in your head and a purpose alive in your daily life.

Professional Concepts Services: Where Purpose Meets Income

"Step Into Success" centers on young people finding their DNA-coded purpose early—before decades of going the wrong way have a chance to harden. "Professional Concepts Services" stretches this work to adults, teams, and leaders.

This is where your DNA-driven purpose meets your bank account. Where we help people turn what they were born to do into money that sustains them. Because purpose without income is just a beautiful dream you can't afford to live.

Street Translation: You shouldn't have to pick between paying your bills and being yourself. Most people accept that split. They work a job that has nothing to do with who they are from nine to five. Then they try to squeeze their real self into nights and weekends until they burn out.

We offer a different equation: what if your work expressed your purpose instead of blocking it? In real life, this looks like the teacher told she should go corporate for the money. She finally builds a career around her gift and finds a money model that works. Or the executive successful at something he was never meant to do. He finally gets the guts and the plan to shift.

Most people work forty years in jobs that have nothing to do with what they were born for. They trade their one-of-a-kind lives for paychecks in careers that slowly wear down their spirits—like water dripping on stone. Not dramatic. Just steady and destructive.

They count down to retirement so they can "finally start living." But by then, their health is gone. Their energy is spent. Their best years built someone else's dream.

We teach a different path. How to get paid for being who you actually are. How to build work around your DNA-coded strengths. Instead of forcing yourself into a role that needs you to pretend eight hours a day.

We offer custom coaching for leaders, teams, and organizations ready for real change. Leadership built on true purpose, not borrowed models that crumble under pressure. Team building based on paired DNA-coded strengths, not personality quizzes people forget by Friday.

Here's the plain truth for leaders: your company's ceiling is set by how many of your people are living their actual DNA-driven purpose.

An accountant who should be an artist will never give you their best. They're burning energy pretending—and that act has an expiration date. A salesperson who belongs in teaching will flame out inside two years. You'll wonder what went wrong. The signs were always there.

We help leaders spot who's aligned and who's not. Make hard calls about fit. Build teams where jobs match genetic design.

This isn't about keeping everyone comfortable. It's about building something that lasts past the next quarter.

Real change doesn't come from posters in the break room or team-building games nobody remembers by Monday lunch. It comes from people learning they're in the wrong spot and having the guts to move. Or learning they're in the right spot and finally bringing everything they have.

Real teams aren't built on goals handed down from above. They're built on purpose alignment. When everyone lives their DNA-driven purpose, you don't have to beg for creativity or force teamwork. It flows. Because people are finally doing what they were made to do.

Inclusive Power

"Step Into Success" is built to reach everyone. All backgrounds. All starting points. But we aim hardest at the people told that purpose is a luxury—reserved for those with different zip codes, different skin, different last names.

We operate from a truth I hold with fierce conviction: every human being carries DNA-coded purpose. Finding that purpose is not a privilege for the lucky few. It is a basic human need and right.

This shapes everything about how we work. The examples we use. How we deliver the content. The cultural awareness needed when serving different communities carrying different histories and wounds.

The core need for purpose is the same everywhere. It's coded in everyone's DNA. But the walls people face, the tools they can reach, and the ways purpose might show up—those change depending on where you're from.

We give special, deliberate focus to communities shut out of self-discovery on purpose. Communities wrecked by poverty that didn't happen by accident. Targeted by systems designed against them. Scarred by violence that became normal. Held back by schools that were never set up to help them rise.

We partner with community groups, churches, schools, and service agencies already trusted in those neighborhoods. You can't drop into someone's block with a workbook and expect them to hand over their purpose. Trust has to be earned. It's earned through relationship.

I've worked in communities where people had never been told they carry something unique. Whole neighborhoods where the message from day one was: survive. Get by. Don't expect more. The first time someone in our program hears "you were designed for something specific"—you can see it land like a seed hitting open ground. Their eyes change. Their posture shifts. It's not magic. It's truth finally reaching someone who's been starved for it.

Street Translation: Purpose doesn't have an income requirement. It doesn't ask what school you went to. It doesn't check your credit score. Your DNA doesn't care about your zip code. The blueprint inside a kid in the projects is just as real and just as divine as the one in the suburbs. The difference isn't design. It's access. That's what we're here to fix.

Reaching Across Ages and Ways of Learning

One standout feature of this program: it meets people where they are. Different ages. Different stages. Different ways of learning.

We work with children as young as eight. That matters deeply. We plant seeds of DNA-driven purpose early. Before the world piles its weight on young shoulders. This helps kids skip the decades of drifting that trap so many adults.

For children, the focus is on exploring natural gifts, building strong identity, and believing they have something real to give. For teens, it shifts to values, identity apart from peer pressure, and early mapping of how their design might become a future. For adults, it tackles mid-life turns, legacy, career shifts, and pulling scattered experiences into one clear expression of purpose.

We offer in-person workshops for people who thrive on shared energy. Virtual groups for those far away. Self-paced online content for odd schedules. Mobile tools for learning in small bites throughout the day. Blended models that mix it all.

No one should miss their purpose because the delivery method didn't fit their life.

Answering the Questions That Keep You Up at Night

This program goes straight at the questions people carry their whole lives. The ones that show up at three in the morning when distraction can't protect you: "What am I here for? What is my purpose? How do I live a life that actually matters?"

We don't hand out cookie-cutter answers that fit everyone and therefore help no one. We give people the tools and support to find their own answers—rooted in their unique DNA-coded design.

Think of it like a combination lock. Everybody's code is different. I can't give you my numbers and expect your lock to open. But I can teach you how locks work. I can show you how to listen for the click. I can stand beside you while you turn the dial. That's what this program does. We don't hand you someone else's answer. We help you find yours.

And we tell the truth most self-help won't: purpose is not a fixed spot where you arrive and coast. Your DNA-driven purpose may expand, deepen, and take new forms across seasons. The core stays. The expression shifts. We teach people to read the signs and adjust— not to abandon their calling, but to let it grow.

The Expanding Impact of Purpose

This work goes way past one person's change. It sends out ripples that become waves, and waves that become tides.

When people find and switch on their DNA-coded purpose, they change everything they touch. Often without realizing it. They bring fresh, electric energy to their families. New creativity to their work. A different way of living that gives others quiet permission to ask: "Am I living outside my own design?"

These personal shifts add up into group change—staggering, almost unbelievable in reach. Companies get sharper when filled with purpose-driven people. Families get warmer when parents model fulfillment instead of quiet suffering. Communities get stronger when people see how their gifts connect to and build up others.

The Collective Vision

The vision for "Step Into Success" is not ego dressed up as charity. I want to be straight about that. Too many mission statements are just ambition wearing a halo.

This is a real, shared mission to help people reach and switch on the full potential coded in their DNA. When we align with what God placed in us before birth, we tap abilities we never knew existed. Things that seemed impossible become daily practice. That's not hype. I've watched it happen in person after person.

This vision pushes back hard against what culture tells us about success. It rejects the idea that worth is set by wealth stacked, status won, or power held. Those markers have nothing to do with who we actually are at our core.

Instead, it paints a picture of human thriving rooted in being real. In expressing DNA-driven purpose. In giving to something bigger than yourself.

The work keeps unfolding with every person who finds their purpose and starts living it. This isn't just my calling. It's an open invitation.

Join a movement toward a world where the 98.5% finally learn what the 1.5% have always known. True fulfillment doesn't come from chasing what the world rewards. It comes from living the purpose written in your genes. Before you drew your first breath. Before anyone told you what to want.

I will spend every day I have left making sure as many people as possible get that invitation—and the tools to accept it.

The Program in Your Pocket

Everything you just read about the three stages—Discover, Define, Develop—is not just a framework sitting on a page. It is a living process that thousands of people are walking through right now, in real time, with tools built specifically for where they are. Not where someone else is. Where they are.

The Step Into Success app was built because one thing became clear early: most people do not fail at finding their purpose because they lack knowledge. They fail because life keeps happening. Monday comes back around. The bills do not pause. The demands do not stop. And the work of excavating who you actually are gets pushed to the back of the line, again and again, until it disappears entirely.

The app changes that. It puts the three-stage framework in your hand in five-minute daily windows that fit inside the life you already have. It gives you the tools to do the digging on a Tuesday morning before work, during a lunch break, in the quiet after everyone else is asleep. It asks you the questions this book has been raising and holds space for the answers long enough for them to mean something.

Think of it like this. This book is the map. It shows you the terrain, names the landmarks, and explains why the path matters. The Step Into Success app is the GPS—the tool that talks you through the route turn by turn, in real time, in the actual conditions of your actual life. You need both.

If you are ready to stop reading about transformation and start living it—if the stone is in your hand and you want to drop it—open the camera on your phone and point it at the code below. The first step has been waiting for you since you opened this book.

CHAPTER 4: THE QUESTION THAT MATTERS MOST — BEYOND STUFF, TOWARD REAL LIFE

There is a question echoing through every life. It follows you from your first clear thought to your last breath. It demands full, undivided attention—yet most of us spend a lifetime running from it.

It goes deeper than the shallow scorecards our culture worships. It's not about bank balances. Not about fame. Not about the pile of stuff that fills garages but leaves hearts hollow.

It's about something far more real, far more worth your limited time: a life filled with genuine fulfillment, deep peace, and honest happiness. A life where you are free to live your DNA-coded purpose.

In our world today, the story of "success" has been squeezed down until there's barely room to breathe inside it. It's been reduced to buying things and getting applause.

Every screen, every billboard, every social feed fires the same message: happiness equals luxury cars, big houses, and vacations posted for strangers' approval.

These messages seep in like water through a crack—slowly, quietly, and with damage you don't see until the foundation is wet. They shape what we chase before we even know we're chasing it.

Then one day we look up and realize we're on a treadmill. Running hard. Going nowhere. Each win brings a quick hit that fades like fog. We're still hungry. Still empty. Still cut off from our DNA-driven purpose.

Street Translation: We're chasing a version of success designed by people who profit from our hunger. The whole consumer machine runs on one lie: what you have isn't enough, and who you are isn't enough.

Every ad whispers: "You're incomplete without this." And we buy it—with our money, our time, our energy, and our purpose. In your real life, this looks like upgrading the car when the old one still runs. Taking the promotion that adds stress and subtracts meaning. Spending Saturday shopping for things you'll forget by Tuesday— while the thing that would actually fill you sits untouched.

We chase houses we can't truly afford. Stack up debt to keep up looks that fool nobody paying real attention. Pursue cars that lose half their value before the first payment clears.

We grab at symbols of status that promise fulfillment but deliver only quick distraction from the nagging sense that something core is missing. Something no purchase can fix.

These visible markers of success turn out to be thin and, in the end, crushing in their emptiness. They can't protect you from depression—which doesn't care about your address. They can't stop the ache of loneliness that finds you in crowded rooms. They can't block addiction's false comfort.

Think about the people who seem to "have it all." Actors on magazine covers. Business giants whose names mean wealth and power. Sports legends who pack stadiums.

We envy their lives—the ones built for cameras and press releases. But behind closed doors, many of them fight a deep, soul-level emptiness. They wonder why success feels so hollow alone at three in the morning when the clapping has stopped.

The news overflows with stories of famous, wealthy people who fall into breakdowns, addiction, even suicide. Stories that should make us question everything we've been taught about what makes a good life.

Robin Williams brought joy to millions with a gift that seemed endless. He fought inner darkness that took his life despite every kind of success the world measures. Anthony Bourdain traveled the globe, dined with presidents, checked every box on society's list—and ended his life in a hotel room.

Kate Spade built a fashion empire with her name on stores worldwide. She still couldn't escape the despair that comes from living cut off from DNA-coded purpose.

These sharp, sobering stories underline a truth you can't argue with: money cannot heal what's broken inside. Outside success cannot fill the hole left by living outside your genetic blueprint for meaning.

Think of it like filling a swimming pool with a garden hose— except the pool has no bottom. You can run that hose for fifty years. You can upgrade to a fire hose. Won't matter. The water goes straight through. That's what chasing money does when purpose is missing. The container can't hold what you're pouring in.

I've watched this in my own circle. Brilliant people burning through win after win but still restless. Still searching. Still filling carts—literal and emotional—hoping the next purchase will finally stick. It never does. The hunger isn't physical. It's spiritual. And spiritual hunger only answers to purpose.

I've sat with people who have everything the world says to want. The house. The car. The title. The portfolio. I've watched them weep because none of it means what they thought. I've also sat with people who own almost nothing by the world's count. They glow with a peace so solid you can almost touch it.

The difference was never money. It was always purpose. Always. No exceptions.

Think too about the countless rich executives working seventy hours a week. Stacking wealth in accounts they rarely check. Meanwhile their marriages crack. Their health breaks down. Their kids grow up knowing their face from photos more than from presence.

These stories show a deep, troubling gap between outside success and inside well-being. Between what society claps for and what the soul calls fulfillment.

Now flip the picture. People who have found deep purpose—who've discovered and lined up with their DNA-driven calling—rarely wrestle with the crushing struggles that haunt people chasing empty awards.

Their lives are anchored in a clear sense of their values, their passions, and their one-of-a-kind gifts. They follow an inner compass pointed at what's real—not what impresses.

I've watched this pattern across every income level and background. People who give themselves to causes bigger than their own comfort carry something different. Teaching kids the world gave up on. Making art that moves hearts in ways money can't touch. Solving problems others walked away from. These people hold a quiet, unshakable peace. No amount of money can buy what they have.

You can see it in how they carry themselves. Their eyes hold the light of purpose being lived, not stuffed down. Their actions flow from an inner well, not outside pressure. There's a gravity to them, a groundedness, that wealth can't fake and status can't copy.

This is why I know—with rock-solid, absolute conviction—that life's greatest treasures can't be bought. Not at any price. Not through any deal.

They are the things that feed your soul and give your days weight and meaning. Experiences that shape who you become. Bonds that enrich your life past any dollar amount.

Moments of joy that steal your breath and remind you what it means to be fully alive. Acts of kindness that ripple outward in ways you'll never fully trace. Love expressed in ways that go past words and touch something eternal. And purpose that fills your life with direction and meaning no title can match.

Picture a child's hug. Small arms wrapped around your neck. A grip that says "you are my whole world." That one moment makes every sacrifice worth it. Or the deep satisfaction of helping someone who truly needs it. Expecting nothing back. Feeling something bloom inside you no paycheck has ever grown.

The thrill of making something beautiful that didn't exist until you created it—a painting, a business, a program, a solution. Or the quiet peace of lying in bed knowing you lived today aligned with your deepest values and DNA-coded purpose.

These experiences create a kind of wealth that grows over time. Unlike stuff that loses value the second you buy it and turns to dust, these treasures last. They become the bedrock of a life well-lived.

Chasing these treasures demands a hard shift in how you see. It's like turning a ship in open water—slow, heavy, but necessary.

It means looking inward for approval instead of outward. Building real self-knowledge instead of a polished image. Putting your DNA-coded values above the ones culture keeps pushing on you.

It means moving past the pull of things that promise fulfillment but only deliver a quick buzz. Reaching instead for the deeper parts of life that connect to your genetic blueprint for meaning.

Street Translation: Self-discovery isn't a spa day. It's surgery. It hurts. It's confusing. There's a recovery time. But the other option is spending your whole life with something inside you that needs to come out.

In real terms, start here: sit down with a notebook. Write the answer to one question: "If money and other people's opinions vanished, what would I do with my life?" Whatever your hand writes before your brain can edit it—that's your starting point. That's your DNA talking.

This path takes courage. Guts to question what everyone accepts as normal. Nerve to admit you may have been chasing the wrong things for years. Willingness to face your deepest fears without the numbing of busyness or distraction.

It demands you fight the stories that keep you running on treadmills going nowhere. Resist the pressure to walk a path that isn't yours just because it's well-worn. Carve your own trail toward the full expression of your genetic design—even when people around you don't get it.

The path may cost you. It may ask for things that seem impossible from where you stand now. But the return is beyond any math.

When your life lines up with your deepest values and DNA-driven purpose, something clicks into place. You feel it in everything—how you wake up, how you work, how you love, how you rest.

Work stops being just a way to pay bills. It becomes a channel for your gifts and a way to give something only you can give. Relationships get deeper and more real—turning from trades into true connection. Free time actually restores you instead of just numbing the ache.

The question we must face—the one that separates lives that matter from lives that just pass time—is not "How much can I earn?" It's not "What will impress people?"

It is: "What is my purpose? What DNA-coded calling am I meant to fulfill in my brief time here?" What unique gifts do I carry that exist in no one else among seven billion? What values ring true at my deepest level when I'm honest? What life do I want when every outside expectation is stripped away and I stand alone with the truth?

Answering takes work. Sustained, focused self-reflection and trying that most people never start because it's uncomfortable and the outcome isn't printed on the box.

It means exploring your passions with honesty. Naming your real strengths without fake modesty. Clearing out your values through tough self-examination that doesn't let you hide behind comfort words.

It means being honest in ways that sting. Facing your limits without excuses. Claiming your potential without hiding behind "I'm not ready yet."

This may mean going back to childhood dreams you dropped for "practical" reasons. Dreams that may have been closer to your DNA-coded purpose than you knew. Dreams your younger self understood before adults taught you to be "realistic."

It may mean breaking free from what others expect. Parents who wanted you to be a doctor. A spouse who needs a certain lifestyle. Peers who grade you by standard measures that have nothing to do with your design.

It may mean dropping society's definition of achievement. The one you've been wearing like clothes that pinch and bind. Clothes everyone calls "appropriate" even though they've never fit. It's time to grab a measure of success that actually fits who you are.

As you dig honestly into this process, refusing to accept shallow answers, you start to find what only you can give. The role you were designed to play in the bigger story.

You uncover where your talents, your fire, and the world's needs cross. The sweet spot where your greatest joy meets the world's greatest need. Where your DNA-coded purpose finds its full, free voice.

This won't always happen in one dramatic flash. It often unfolds slowly—like a photo developing in your hands. Through experiments and watching. Reflecting and adjusting. Course corrections that bring the picture into sharper focus step by step.

Once you see your DNA-driven purpose clearly, you can start the vital work of matching your actions to your values. Not just talking about them at dinner. Actually living them.

You can build a life that fills you personally and matters to others. A life that counts beyond your own comfort. A life that gives back.

This alignment demands intentional, often hard choices. Steady action kept up over time even when obstacles make you question everything.

Look at your work, your relationships, your habits, your surroundings with unflinching honesty. Make changes to bring them in line with your DNA-coded purpose—even when those changes hurt.

That might mean leaving a career that gives safety and status but no meaning. Ending a draining relationship. Moving to a place better suited to your growth—even when it means walking away from what's familiar into what's unknown.

I won't pretend these choices are easy. I've made some of them. The night before a major career change, I sat at my kitchen table at midnight staring at a blank wall. My stomach was in knots. Every voice in my head screamed "stay safe." But a quieter voice—the one that had been whispering for years—said "go." I went. It was the hardest and the best decision of my life.

Here's the thing about scary decisions: they only look impossible from the side you're standing on. Once you step across, you wonder why you waited so long. It's like jumping into a cold pool. Every nerve says don't. But once you're in? Your body adjusts. You start swimming. And you realize the fear was bigger than the water ever was.

It also means building new skills. Creating habits that serve your future self, not just today's comfort. Investing time in training to express your gifts at the highest level. Setting up daily practices that feed your body, mind, and spirit—building the base for a purpose-driven life that can handle storms.

Purpose is not a solo sport. It's a team game. You can't do it sealed off from others, no matter how independent you think you are.

It is a shared experience. Building real bonds. Giving to something bigger than yourself. Seeing that we're all connected in ways both visible and hidden.

Our DNA-driven purposes cross paths and grow stronger when we come together on purpose. Our choices ripple far past what we can see. Our lives can leave a mark that lasts long after we're gone.

When we live with purpose, lined up with our genetic design instead of fighting it, we naturally seek out others who share our values. We build communities of support where people push and lift each other to grow—not compete for scraps.

These bonds create the right soil for purpose to grow and spread instead of dying alone.

Living with purpose also pulls you into the wider world with greater intention. You see that your well-being is deeply tied to others' well-being. Pure selfishness defeats itself—you can't truly thrive while those around you suffer.

Through your work, your involvement, your creativity, your relationships—you try to leave things better than you found them. To give lasting value in whatever corner of the world you fill.

The things that truly matter when you stand at the end of your days looking back? They're not stuff. They're not trophies collecting dust.

They are inner peace that can't be bought at any price. Genuine love that changes both giver and receiver. Purpose aligned with your DNA, not borrowed from others. And a life that fills you and helps others in ways that echo for generations.

When we shift focus from outside to inside—from things to meaning—we wake up the true potential sleeping inside us. When we stop chasing what impresses others and start serving our DNA-coded purpose, everything changes.

We can help build a world where everyone gets a real shot. The joy, the peace, the deep fulfillment that comes from living the purpose written in your genes. Before birth. Before conditioning. Before the world told them who to be.

The road ahead is not about being perfect. That's not possible and not needed. It's about progress. Honest, messy, steady progress.

Taking one step at a time toward your DNA-driven purpose. Not waiting for certainty first—because certainty doesn't come before the first step. It comes after.

Learning from mistakes instead of freezing because of them. Growing through challenges instead of being crushed. Changing as life gets complex instead of hiding in safe patterns that produce nothing.

Finding joy now—not after the next win. Seeing beauty around you with fresh eyes. Building deep gratitude for the gifts you carry. Especially the gift of purpose coded in your DNA. Waiting to be found. Waiting to be lived.

In the end, we look back at everything. Every choice. Every risk. Every brave moment and every scared one. The question that matters isn't "What did I get?" It isn't "How much did I stack up?"

It's: "What did I give? What did I add during my brief time here? How did I make a difference that lines up with the purpose in my DNA?"

By focusing on giving over getting. Serving others over serving only ourselves. Living a purpose-driven life instead of just collecting things until the clock runs out.

That's how we access life's true wealth—a wealth that goes past anything you can hold in your hands. A wealth measured not by what we owned but by what we gave. Not by what we stacked up but by what we stirred to life in ourselves and lit in others.

That is the legacy worth building. That is the life worth living. And it starts—it has always started—with the purpose written in your DNA.

Before you go to Chapter 5, I want you to answer one question in writing. Thirty seconds. No overthinking.

If someone who loves you completely had to describe what you were built for — not what you do for money, what you were built for — what would they say?

Write it. Even if it stings. Especially if it stings.

That answer is the starting point for everything Chapter 5 is about to show you.

CHAPTER 5: THE ESSENCE OF BEING – PURPOSE AS IDENTITY

Stage 1 – Discover: Excavating What Was Always True

Let me ask you a question that's going to sting.

What do you do?

Now answer a harder one: Who are you?

If those two answers don't match—if who you are at your core has nothing to do with what you spend forty hours a week doing—you're paying a tax most people never talk about. And 98.5% of people are paying it right now.

Not a money tax. Deeper than that. You're paying with your energy. Your health. Your sleep. The look on your face when Sunday night rolls around. You're paying with the version of yourself that never gets to show up—because the role you're playing has nothing to do with the person you were built to be.

This chapter is about finding that person. The real one. The one underneath all the job titles, the expectations, the decisions you made when you were too young or too scared to know better.

And I need you to know this: what you're about to read isn't theory. It's not a framework I found in a textbook.

I found it on a table in an emergency room with twelve minutes of no air in my lungs from 3 **Pulmonary Embolisms** (Blood Clots in the Lungs).

That distance has a price tag. It is staggering—almost impossible to wrap your mind around when you actually sit with the full weight of it—because 98.5% of people are paying it every single day, in every waking hour, in every decision shaped by a self-concept that was built for them rather than by them. They pay it in the form of a specific, chronic exhaustion that no amount of sleep fully addresses—the exhaustion that comes not from doing too much but from doing the wrong things, from spending the finite hours of a finite life maintaining a performance that was never supposed to be the whole story. They pay it in the low-grade restlessness that follows them from job to job, city to city, relationship to relationship, the feeling that the next thing will finally be the right thing—and it never quite is, because the problem was never the thing. The problem was the distance between the thing and the person inside it.

This book exists because that distance can be closed. Not by finding the right job title or the right city or the right set of circumstances— those are all surface-level adjustments that leave the root condition untouched. The distance closes when a person does the deep, honest, often uncomfortable work of excavating what has always been true about them beneath the layers of what other people needed them to be. That excavation is Stage 1 of the purpose framework. It is called Discover, and it is not a passive process of waiting for revelation. It is active. It is on purpose. And it begins with understanding why the excavation is necessary in the first place.

The Debris That Covers the Truth

Every person who comes into this world arrives carrying a specific, one of a kind genetic design—a combination of gifts, passions, perspectives, and capacities that exists nowhere else on earth and was never meant to be replicated. The purpose encoded in that DNA is not a vague spiritual concept. It is as real and as particular as a fingerprint. It is the precise make-up of who this person is at the deepest level, the thing that makes their contribution to the world something only they can make. And it arrives complete. At birth. Before any conditioning has taken place, before any external pressure has been applied, before the world has had a single opportunity to tell this human being who they should be instead.

Then the debris begins to arrive. It comes in layers—some layers laid down with love, some with fear, some with cultural pressure so normalized that no one questions it as pressure at all. Parents, doing their best with what they know, begin the shaping. 'You're so good at math—you should be an engineer.' 'Artists don't make money.' 'Be practical.' 'Stop dreaming.' 'That's not realistic.' Teachers add their layers. 'You're not performing up to your potential in this subject'— the subject that happens to have nothing to do with what this child was actually built for. Peers add their layers. The culture adds its layers—entire value systems about what constitutes a worthy life, a successful person, a respectable contribution. By the time most people reach adulthood, the original design is buried under decades of piled up debris, and the person walking around in the world has no clear connection to the truth that was there from the beginning.

Think about what an archaeologist does when they arrive at a site that holds something significant. They don't walk up to the ground, see a surface that looks like every other surface, and conclude there is nothing there. They know that what matters most is what's underneath. They bring tools designed not for construction but for careful, patient removal—brushes and picks and sieves, instruments made specifically for clearing away what piled up over time without damaging what was always there. The work is not glamorous. It is slow. It requires the ability to handle what looks like nothing with the attention and care you would give to something precious, because you know that what you're looking for is there, waiting, just under the surface. You cannot rush it. You cannot force it. You can only keep clearing, carefully and honestly, until the truth begins to emerge.

I know this because I did the dig myself. Not by choice. Not on a quiet weekend with a journal and good coffee.

Because twelve minutes *without breath in my body* ripped away every layer at once.

Most people get to excavate slowly. A year of therapy here. A hard conversation there. A season where everything stops making sense. They peel back one layer at a time.

I got dynamite.

When they brought me back, I didn't have the option of going back to the performance. The layers were gone. All of them. And what I found underneath all that rubble was the same thing you're going to find underneath yours.

The original design. Still there. Still intact. Still waiting.

That's what Stage 1 is about. Not building something new. Uncovering what was already built.

Stage 1 is digging work. The 'site' is you. The debris is everything that was layered on top of your DNA-encoded truth over the course of your life—every expectation absorbed, every dream edited for practicality, every gift suppressed because the environment you were in didn't know what to do with it. The tools are honesty, reflection, and the willingness to stay with the discomfort of not having immediate answers. And what you are looking for—your purpose, your one of a kind design, the specific truth about who you are and what you were built to contribute—has been there the entire time. It did not leave. It did not expire. It waited.

Here is the theory behind why most people never start the excavation: the debris does not feel like debris. It feels like identity. The career chosen at twenty-two under pressure from parents who were managing their own fear—after fifteen years, that career doesn't feel like a costume. It feels like a self. The degree pursued to satisfy someone else's definition of a worthy path—after years of building credentials around it, it doesn't feel like a layer imposed from outside.

It feels like the foundation. The personality adaptations made to survive a classroom, a household, a workplace that wasn't designed for who this person actually was—those adaptations, after enough repetition, stop feeling like adaptations. They feel like character. And this is exactly why the excavation is hard. You are not digging through things that feel foreign. You are digging through things that feel like you.

In your actual life, this is what the beginning of Stage 1 feels like: it feels like instability. The career that felt like your identity starts to feel like a costume, and that shift is disorienting before it is liberating. The degree that felt like your foundation starts to feel like someone else's foundation, and that recognition can produce grief before it produces clarity. The personality you've been presenting to the world for decades starts to feel like a performance, and the exposure of that performance—even to yourself, even in the privacy of genuine reflection—can feel threatening before it feels like freedom. This is normal. This is not a sign that something is going wrong. This is the feeling of debris beginning to shift.

The Costume and What It Costs

Most people who are disconnected from their DNA-encoded purpose are wearing what I call a costume. Not a dramatic disguise that fools no one—nothing as obvious as that. The costume looks like a professional identity. It looks like a LinkedIn profile and a morning routine and a carefully maintained persona that presents the version of this person that the world has agreed to accept. The costume can be genuinely impressive. Other people see it and feel admiration, even envy. The person wearing it receives the admiration and feels—in the same moment—the specific hollowness of being praised for something that isn't quite real. Because they know, somewhere underneath the performance, that what is being celebrated is the costume and not the person inside it.

The physical cost of wearing the costume is something that most writing about purpose glosses over in favor of more comfortable language about potential and possibility, but I am going to say it plainly because I have felt it in my own body and watched it in the bodies of people I have worked with across every age and background. The costume has weight. Real weight. It lives in the muscles that are constantly braced for the next performance. In the jaw that is never quite relaxed because relaxation means dropping the mask and dropping the mask is not safe. In the shoulders that carry the specific tension of a person who is always, at some level, managing—managing their presentation, managing other people's perceptions, managing the constant low-level anxiety of being found out as something other than what they've claimed to be. This is not metaphor. This is the physical signature of a life lived outside of DNA alignment.

There is no more accurate image for living outside your DNA-encoded purpose than trying to work a lock with the wrong key. You can get remarkably skilled at it—the right pressure, the right angle, the particular finesse that comes from years of practice with this specific mismatch. You can develop a technique for almost making it work. And some people do. They build entire careers, entire lives, on the almost—on the version of success that is achieved through sheer skill at working against the grain of what they actually are. But here is what the wrong key always costs, regardless of how skilled the hand holding it becomes: something takes damage. The key bends a little more each time. The lock wears unevenly. The mechanism that was designed to respond to the right key becomes increasingly resistant to everything because it has been worked too long by something it was never built to recognize. That damage accumulates. And it shows up—in the body, in the spirit, in the specific quality of emptiness that follows even genuine achievement when the achievement is built on the wrong foundation.

The student who graduates at the top of a program that was chosen for them rather than by them holds their diploma with a smile that doesn't reach the eyes, because somewhere in the body is the knowledge that the achievement, real as it is, belongs to a version of themselves they didn't choose. The professional who receives the promotion they worked years for goes home that night and feels—beneath the celebration, beneath the genuine pride—a quietness that shouldn't be there. The parent who has given everything to building a life for their family looks up one morning to find that the life they built doesn't quite fit the person who built it. These are not failures. These are the most honest signals a human being can receive, and they are the entry point into Stage 1.

The Invitation to Start Digging

Stage 1 begins not with an answer but with a question—and not a comfortable question. It begins with the willingness to ask, honestly and without the protection of a predetermined answer: Who am I when I am not performing? What is actually in me, underneath all of it, that was there before the world started shaping me and will be there when all the shaping is stripped away? What energizes me in a way that doesn't feel like motivation—that feels like coming alive? What makes me angry in a way that contains a clue about what I was built to care about? What have I dismissed as impractical or unrealistic that keeps returning, in the quiet, like something that refuses to stop being true?

These are not just nice-sounding questions. They are the tools. And the answers — when a person pursues them with real honesty rather than the kind of self-reflection that stops the moment it gets uncomfortable — do not arrive as grand revelations that rearrange everything in a single moment. They arrive as patterns. As recurring themes in what a person finds genuinely absorbing versus what they find merely tolerable. As the specific quality of aliveness that shows up in some experiences and is entirely absent from others. As the thread that runs through every version of themselves across every season of their life, the thing that was true at twelve and true at twenty-five and true at forty and is still true now, underneath everything that was built on top of it.

The Discover stage is the commitment to following that thread. Not to a destination—Stage 1 does not deliver a finished answer. It delivers a direction. A cleared path. The beginning of the excavation that, pursued with honesty and courage, eventually reveals the specific, one of a kind genetic design that has been waiting inside this human being the entire time—not as something new to become, but as something old and true to finally stop running from.

Stage 2 – Define: The Declaration That Changes Everything

Once the excavation begins—once a person clears enough debris to catch a glimpse of what has always been underneath—the next question arrives, and it is both simple and terrifying in equal measure: now what do you do with what you find? Insight without declaration is archaeology without structure. You can dig all the way to the original foundation and still choose to build the same house on top of it. Stage 2 exists to close that gap. It is the stage where what has been uncovered gets declared—first internally, then externally, then repeatedly, in small moments and large ones, until the declaration stops being an act of courage and becomes simply the truth of how this person moves through the world.

The shift from Doing to Being is the central movement of Stage 2, and it deserves more than a sentence because most people have spent their entire lives on the wrong side of it without ever having it named. Doing is performing your purpose as an activity—something you start and stop, something you can leave at the office, something that exists in certain contexts and disappears in others. Being is living your DNA-encoded purpose as an identity—something that runs underneath everything, that informs every interaction whether you're working or resting, that shapes how you move through a room and what you notice and what you care about and what you cannot stop caring about no matter how many times you tell yourself it isn't practical.

Think about what it means to say 'I teach' versus 'I am a teacher.' Those two sentences look almost identical on a page. They live in completely different worlds. 'I teach' is a function. You can perform that function for twenty years, walk out of the building at four o'clock, and leave it behind entirely. It's a coat—you put it on in the morning and hang it on the door at night, and it's just hanging there, waiting for whoever needs to wear it next. 'I am a teacher' is not a coat. That is skin. You do not leave skin at the office. The person who is a teacher in their DNA does not stop teaching when the classroom empties. They are teaching at dinner, in conversation, in the way they explain things to strangers, in the particular quality of attention they bring to anyone who is trying to learn something. Because the purpose encoded in their genetic design does not clock out. It runs twenty-four hours a day whether it is being compensated or not.

Here is the theory that drives Stage 2: the Define stage is not about choosing a new path. It is about declaring who you already are. The difference between those two things is the difference between the 98.5% and the 1.5%. The 98.5% spend their lives choosing paths— the practical path, the safe path, the path that satisfies whoever is watching—because they have not yet made the prior declaration about who they are at the level of their genetic design. Without that declaration, every path is just a path. With it, the path forward is not chosen. It is recognized.

In your actual life, Stage 2 looks like this: it is the career professional in their mid-forties who stops adding credentials to the resume that describes what they can do and starts building toward the work that matches what they were encoded to do—and feels, for the first time, that the effort is going somewhere real. It is the student who stops optimizing their academic performance for a future they were assigned and starts asking, with genuine curiosity and without the filter of practicality, what they would pursue if the only criterion was alignment with their actual design. It is the parent who looks at the life they have built—a good life, a solid life, a life that serves everyone around them—and decides that modeling quiet desperation for their children is not the legacy they intended, and begins the work of becoming a person whose children will grow up knowing what it looks like to live from the inside out. Each of these is a Declaration. Each of them is the beginning of Stage 2.

The Metamorphosis: What the Body Knows Before the Mind Admits It

I want to spend real time on the physical dimension of this shift, because the literature on purpose tends to live entirely in the intellectual register—reorganizing values, clarifying goals, reframing narratives—as if the body is a passive bystander in the process of becoming who you were designed to be. It is not a bystander. The body has been tracking the being off track the entire time, logging every day spent in the wrong costume, recording every moment of performance with the specific physical signature of maintained being fake. And when the Define stage takes hold—when the declaration becomes real—the body is the first place the change shows up.

The old identity has weight. This is not a metaphor—it is a measurable, physical reality. The tension that lives permanently in the shoulders of a person who is always performing is the muscular cost of maintaining a presentation. It does not release fully in sleep because sleep doesn't switch off the underlying identity management. The breath that sits high and shallow in the chest of someone living outside their DNA alignment is the body's response to a life that requires constant vigilance—constant monitoring of how the performance is being received, constant adjustment for what the room needs, constant suppression of the authentic responses that would break the character. The jaw that never quite unclenches. The constant alertness that masquerades as professionalism. The specific quality of post-performance exhaustion that follows not from doing too much but from being someone you are not, hour after hour, day after day, year after year.

I know what this feels like because I lived inside it for years. I had roles that looked significant from the outside and felt hollow from the inside—roles with titles and responsibilities and external markers of progress that should have produced satisfaction and instead produced a specific, chronic emptiness I could not explain to anyone who hadn't felt it. Every morning I put on the costume of what I was supposed to be. Every night I took it off. And in the quiet between those two moments—the moment after the mask came down and before the demand to put it back up arrived—there was a gap that never closed, a distance between the performance and the person performing it that got louder with every passing year, no matter how well the performance was received.

Think about a blacksmith and fire. Fire applied to the wrong metal does not produce anything useful—it destroys. It warps. It burns through what was there and leaves a ruin of what might have been. The heat is real, the intensity is real, and the damage is real, regardless of the skill or the intention of the person applying it. But fire applied to the right metal, in the hands of someone who knows what they are working with, does something entirely and completely different. The same heat that would wreck the wrong material transforms the right material into something stronger and more precise and more capable than it could ever have been without passing through the fire. Your DNA-encoded purpose is the iron. The trials, the failures, the years of confusion and being off track—those are the fire. Living outside your purpose means the fire is burning the wrong thing. And you feel every degree of it. Stage 2 is when the alignment happens—when the iron and the fire find each other—and when what was destroying you begins, for the first time, to refine you.

When the Define stage begins to take hold in a person's life, the first physical signal is almost always the breath. It drops. Suddenly and noticeably, it drops from the high, shallow holding pattern of the performed life into something lower and fuller—a breath that actually reaches the bottom of the lungs because the bottom of the lungs is no longer braced against the threat of being found out. The shoulders follow. Not because anyone gave permission to relax—but because the muscular work of maintaining the performance has been released at the source. The jaw unclenches. The eyes change quality—from the carefully managed, room-monitoring expression of someone who is always performing, to something more direct and more present and more honest. These are not small changes. In a human face, these changes are unmistakable. The people who love this person notice them before this person has said a single word about what has shifted.

The Purpose Level: Living From the Inside Out

The Purpose Level is the term for the state that Stage 2 moves a person toward—the state of being where what you do in the world is no longer a performance of your identity but a direct, unfiltered expression of it. It is the point at which the costume and the skin become the same thing, not because the person has stopped being professional or strategic or on purpose, but because the strategy and the on purposeness are now in service of who they actually are rather than who they have been pretending to be. At the Purpose Level, the split closes. The professional self and the private self stop being two different people managed separately, and become one person moving through the world with the specific, unusual quality of coherence that only comes from full alignment between the inside and the outside.

Here is what the Purpose Level is not: it is not a state of ease. It is not the absence of difficulty or the elimination of challenge. Life does not get easier at the Purpose Level. What changes is the texture of the hard. Before alignment, every challenge is a drain—you are fighting uphill in shoes that don't fit, spending energy you never get back just to maintain the performance on top of doing the actual work. After alignment, challenges feel different. They feel like resistance that is working you in the right direction—the way a muscle works when it lifts something heavy in the correct posture. The effort is real. Sometimes it is harder than the comfortable performance it replaced. But it is effort that builds something, that compounds rather than depletes, that produces genuine satisfaction rather than the hollow relief of having survived another round of being someone you are not.

A river with one clear source moves with force and direction. It knows where it is going because it knows exactly where it comes from, and that certainty translates directly into momentum—the water cuts through whatever is in front of it because there is no ambiguity about the direction, no energy lost to internal conflict about which way to flow. Now imagine a river being pulled from three different sources at the same time—a person's work identity pulling one way, their home identity pulling another, their inner life pulling a third, and the version of themselves that different audiences need pulling in a dozen more directions on top of those. That river does not move forward with force. It spreads out. It loses depth. It turns muddy from the collision of its own contradictory currents. The energy is technically still there, but it is going nowhere that matters, because it is being consumed entirely by its own internal conflict.

Most people are the second river. The energy cost of carrying two versions of themselves through the world—the one that shows up at work and the one that exists at home, the one that performs for audiences and the one that exists in the quiet—is staggering, almost impossible to calculate, because it is so deeply built into the structure of daily life that it has stopped registering as a cost at all. It just feels like normal. It just feels like this is what it costs to be an adult, to be responsible, to manage the complexity of a life that touches many different people with many different needs. Stage 2 is the stage that collapses the split. Not by eliminating complexity, but by giving every context the same source—by running one current through every room, every role, every relationship, so that the energy that was being consumed by the split becomes available for the work that actually matters.

When Purpose Becomes the Person: Service Without Force

Something happens at the Purpose Level that almost no one predicts and almost everyone who reaches it is surprised by: the work stops being about the person doing it. Not because they decided to be selfless—not because they made a strategic choice to prioritize service over self-interest. It happens the way a lit candle produces heat and light—not as a decision the candle makes each morning, but as the natural output of what a candle fundamentally is. When a person is living from their DNA-encoded purpose, contribution becomes the natural output of their being. They are not performing service. They are simply being what they are, fully, in the world, and what they are happens to be exactly what other people need.

In your actual life, this is what that shift looks like: the enormous willpower required to be the person you were trying to be when you were living outside alignment—the constant reminders, the manufactured motivation, the daily effort of sustaining a commitment that never felt natural because it was built on a foundation that wasn't yours—most of that disappears. Not because you became less disciplined. Because the discipline is no longer fighting against the grain of who you actually are. The person you were trying to be and the person you actually are have, finally, become the same person. And when those two things come together, the energy that was being spent on the gap between them becomes available for something else—for the work, for the people, for the specific contribution that only this one human being was encoded to make.

This is the core promise of Stage 2, stated plainly: you do not have to become someone different. You have to stop being someone you're not.

Read that again. Slowly.

Because this is the part where most people waste years. They go back to school for a new degree. They read every book on reinvention. They create vision boards and five-year plans. And none of it sticks. Because you can't build on top of a false foundation.

The clarity I found on that table was exactly this: the performance was exhausting because it was a performance. The real thing doesn't cost that much energy. It comes easy. That's how you know it's yours.

That shift—from the performed identity to the declared identity to the lived identity—is the whole work of Define. And it is the foundation on which everything in Stage 3 is built. Because you cannot develop what you have not yet declared. You cannot build a life around a purpose you have not yet claimed as yours. The declaration is not the end of the work. It is the beginning of the kind of work that actually has somewhere real to go.

Before you turn this page, I need you to do one thing. It takes sixty seconds.

Grab whatever's closest — a pen, your phone, the margin right here. Write down one word that describes what you found in this chapter. Not a sentence. One word. The thing you've been doing that isn't actually you. Write it.

Now write the one word for what IS you. The real version. The one that comes easy.

Those two words are your compass for Chapter 6. Everything that follows is built on the distance between them.

We're almost there.

78

CHAPTER 6: THE MISSION TO TRANSFORM – DEVELOP, SERVE, AND MULTIPLY

Stage 3 – Develop: Where Identity Meets the World

Discover unearths the truth. Define declares it. But neither of those stages changes what a person's Monday morning looks like. Neither pays a bill, builds an organization, raises a child with intention, or makes a contribution that outlasts the person making it. That is the territory of Stage 3—and it is the stage where the purpose framework stops being idea-based and starts being gut-levelly, practically real. Develop is where the declared identity meets the economy. Where what you now know yourself to be gets expressed outward, into the structures of daily life, into the marketplace, into the communities and families and institutions that are waiting—whether they know it or not—for this specific person to finally show up as who they actually are.

This is also the stage that most people who made it through excavation and declaration either resist or rush. They resist it because Stage 3 asks something different than the first two stages asked. Discover required honesty. Define required courage. Develop requires sustained, disciplined work across time—the willingness to look honestly at the gap between who you now know yourself to be and what you currently have the skill, the knowledge, and the resources to do, and to close that gap day after day, without the emotional intensity of a breakthrough to carry you. The seed knows what it was designed to become. The soil, the water, the light, the time—none of that is automatic. It has to be arranged, tended, and protected. That is Stage 3.

The Cost of Standing Still: What Happens When the Develop Stage Never Comes

There is a kind of slow shrinking that happens when a person excavates the truth of who they are, catches a genuine glimpse of their DNA-encoded purpose, makes the internal declaration—and then doesn't act. Doesn't develop. Doesn't close the gap between the identity they've claimed and the life that expresses it. It is, in some ways, a more painful version of the original disconnection, because now the person knows what they're missing. Before Stage 1, the numbness was total. You can be numb to something you've never felt. But once you have touched the truth of your genetic design—once you have felt, even briefly, the specific aliveness that comes from being fully who you are—going back to the performance is no longer neutral. It is a choice. And the body keeps score of that choice in a way it never did before.

Think about a pond with no inlet and no outlet. From a distance it looks peaceful—smooth surface, still water, no visible disturbance. But a stagnant pond and a still pond are not the same thing, and what lives in them is not the same thing, and what they do to everything around them is not the same thing. A pond with real flow—water moving in, moving through, moving out—is alive in ways that are invisible from the surface but unmistakable once you know what to look for. Things grow in it because there is oxygen. Things breathe in it because the water is moving. It connects to something larger than itself and that connection is what makes it life-giving rather than merely decorative. A stagnant pond has the same surface. Underneath, the oxygen is gone. Things die in stagnant water, quietly and without announcement, not because anything dramatic happened but simply because the conditions for life stopped being present.

The person who discovers their DNA-encoded purpose and does not develop it becomes a stagnant pond. Not through failure—through doing nothing. The gifts are still there. The truth that was uncovered in Stage 1 is still there. The declaration made in Stage 2 is still real. But without the outlet of Stage 3—without the disciplined, practical work of building the skills and structures and relationships that allow the purpose to actually flow into the world—the oxygen runs out. The contribution that only this one person could have made begins to weaken. The version of themselves that was possible grows quiet. And the specific, staggering cost of that silence is paid not just by this person but by every individual who would have been changed by the contribution that never came.

Here is the truth about doing nothing that rarely gets said plainly: the world is measurably poorer for every person who dies with their DNA-driven purpose still undeveloped inside them. Not metaphorically poorer. Actually poorer. The teacher who never taught the students only they could have reached. The builder who never built the thing only their particular combination of gifts could have produced. The leader who never led the people who needed exactly their kind of leadership. The parent who modeled quiet endurance instead of full aliveness, and whose children absorbed that model as the definition of what adult life requires. These are not abstract losses. They are real and specific and permanent. Stage 3 is the cure. It is not optional—not for the person, and not for the world that is waiting for what only they can give.

The Ripple That Starts at Home

When a person moves through all three stages—when they discover who they actually are, declare it, and begin developing the life that expresses it—the transformation is never contained to the individual. It moves outward. Immediately and always. The people who live closest to this person are the first to feel it, often before they have words for what has changed, often before the person undergoing the change has words for it either. Partners notice first, in the particular quality of presence that comes home from certain conversations and certain work—not just physically in the room, but actually there, eyes present, mind not managing the gap between the performance and the person underneath it. The weight that was being carried invisibly—the weight of the wrong life, the cost of the daily costume—begins to lift, and the space it occupied becomes available for something that was not possible before: genuine connection, uncarefully chosen and unperformed.

Children watch all of this and understand it in a way they cannot yet say. This is the most important thing to say about the ripple effect on family, and it deserves to be said without softening: children do not listen to what parents tell them about life. They watch what parents do with theirs. A child who grows up in a household where the adults are performing lives that don't fit them absorbs a specific, burned into them about what adulthood requires—that the price of responsibility is to stop being real, that the dreams you had when you were young are things you eventually put away, that joy is a weekend thing, that the question of what you were born to do is a luxury that practical people cannot afford. That lesson is not spoken. It is lived. And it is learned, in the marrow, in a way that no speech or lecture can undo.

But a child who watches a parent find their DNA-driven purpose and actually develop it—who grows up in a household where someone they love is visibly, unmistakably becoming who they were designed to be—learns something entirely different. They learn that there is a version of adulthood where what you do and who you are can be the same thing. They learn to take their own gifts seriously because they watched someone take theirs seriously. They develop a tolerance for the discomfort of growth that children who watched only endurance never develop. They grow up with something most children never have: a model. A living, breathing, daily demonstration that the question of what you were born to do is not a luxury. It is the whole point. And that model—that single transformed life expressing its full DNA-driven purpose—changes the path of every life it touches, including lives that will never know where the change began.

Edification of Education©: The Re-Coding of How You Learn

The conventional education system was built for a purpose, and that purpose was not individual DNA alignment. It was built to produce predictable outputs at scale—workers who could follow instructions, citizens who understood the rules of the existing structure, people equipped to fill roles that had already been designed by someone else. That system has produced genuinely useful things. What it has never produced, and was never designed to produce, is a person who is fully alive to the particular, one of a kind purpose that their specific genetic make-up was built to express. The gap it leaves is real. And most people spend their adult lives compensating for that gap with degrees and credentials and professional development programs that add information to an already overloaded mind without ever addressing the underlying being off track between what this person knows and what this person was designed to do with what they know.

Let me tell you what the Edification of Education© actually is.

It's not more school. It's not another certification or a second degree.

We flip the script on how you learn.

Right now, most people learn the way they were told to learn in school: sit down, take in information, pass the test. The problem is that almost none of that information has anything to do with the specific thing your DNA was built to do. You end up full of facts that point in every direction but yours.

Aimed education is different. Every book you read, every class you take, every skill you build — it all points at one thing. The thing you were designed for. You're not stuffing your head with information anymore. You're arming yourself for a specific mission.

Think of a soldier preparing for a specific operation. He doesn't study everything. He studies what he needs for that hill, that building, that mission. His education has a target.

That's what we build here. Not more knowledge. Pointed knowledge.

Here is the theory, stated clearly: when knowledge is in service of your DNA-driven purpose rather than in service of maintaining a life that doesn't fit, the same information that used to feel like a burden becomes a precision tool. Sharp. Purposeful. Yours. The person who has always been intelligent but has never felt capable is not lacking intelligence—they have been applying intelligence to the wrong frame. Re-coding the frame changes everything about how that intelligence moves through the world. What Edification of Education© produces is not a longer resume. It is a learner who knows, for the first time, exactly what they are learning for.

Professional Economics©: DNA-Economic Alignment

Most people carry what I call Economic Friction. It is the grinding, invisible resistance that shows up when a person tries to build financial stability on a foundation that was never designed to hold the weight of who they actually are. The work generates income—sometimes significant income. The credentials are real. The hours are real. The results, measured by the metrics everyone agrees to use, are real. But the foundation is sand. And the person building on that foundation carries a quiet, persistent sense of shakiness that no amount of income or accomplishment fully dissolves—not because the work is poor quality, but because the work is disconnected from the DNA-driven purpose that would make it feel like more than maintenance. They are not building a life. They are managing one. And there is a difference between those two things that money alone cannot close.

Think about a compass in a storm. The storm is real—the wind, the rain, the loss of visibility, the very reasonable fear that the ground under your feet is not where you thought it was. All of that is real. But the compass does not care about the storm. The compass knows one thing with absolute certainty, regardless of conditions, regardless of how loud the noise around it gets: it knows which way is north. A person who has achieved DNA-economic alignment has that compass. Not a plan—a compass. Plans fail. Plans require conditions that the world is not obligated to provide. But a compass works in every condition, including the ones you didn't plan for, because it is tuned to something deeper than circumstance. Professional Economics© is the framework that builds the compass. The storm doesn't stop. You just stop being lost in it.

Here is the theory behind DNA-economic alignment, stated plainly: when the work you do to generate income is a direct expression of the purpose encoded in your genetic design, the economic output changes in quality, not just quantity.

When your work comes from alignment, people can tell.

Not because you marketed yourself better. Not because your website is cleaner or your LinkedIn is sharper.

Because there's a quality to work done from the right place that can't be faked. It has weight. It has consistency. It has something underneath it that people feel even when they can't name it.

Think of two singers. One hits every note perfectly. Technically flawless. You can tell they're good. The other one is maybe not as perfect — but every word means something. You can feel it in the room. That's not technique. That's truth.

Your customers feel the difference. Your team feels it. Your audience feels it.

That's what the Professional Frequency is. Not a concept. Not a marketing strategy. It's what happens when what you do lines up with who you are.

When I was on that table, I wasn't thinking about my professional brand. But I'll tell you this — the work I've done since that table has a different quality than the work I did before it. Because I stopped performing. Your people will feel that difference before you even say a word.

It draws differently than work produced from being off track. It compounds differently. It creates the kind of professional reputation that is not manufactured through positioning or personal branding, but earned through the specific, one of a kind quality of a person who is doing exactly the work they were designed to do.

In your actual life, DNA-economic alignment looks like this: the effort required to present yourself professionally stops feeling like performance and starts feeling like clarity. You are not marketing a version of yourself that is slightly larger or slightly more polished than the real thing—you are simply showing the world exactly what you are, and finding that what you actually are is more compelling than anything you could have invented. Opportunities that used to require you to pursue them begin to find you, not through magic but through the simple fact that a clear signal draws matching responses the way a tuning fork draws its frequency from the air around it—not through effort but through being precisely and completely what it is. Participants who complete Professional Economics© do not leave with a better resume. They leave with a retuned professional frequency—and that frequency changes not just how they pursue their work, but what their work, over time, pursues them.

The Ripple: One Transformed Life, Multiplied

When a single stone drops into still water, the ripple it creates does not stop at the edge of the stone's impact. It moves outward in every direction at the same time, growing wider with each second, reaching surfaces the stone itself never touched, carrying the energy of that single drop of contact far beyond anything the stone could have predicted or controlled. This is the physics of what happens when one person fully discovers, declares, and develops their DNA-driven purpose. The transformation does not stay inside them. It cannot stay inside them. It is, by nature, outward-moving—touching the people closest first, then the communities those people inhabit, then the institutions those communities build, then the generations those institutions shape.

This is not idealism. This is how transformation has always actually worked, at every scale, across every era of human history. It has never started at the top with a policy or a system or a grand initiative handed down from authority. It has always started with an individual who did the hard, honest work of becoming fully who they were designed to be, and whose full aliveness gave other people the permission and the model to do the same. One person steps into their DNA-driven purpose. The people around them watch and begin to ask the question for themselves. Those people step into theirs. Each ripple generates new ripples. The pond that was stagnant begins to move. The oxygen returns. The things that were quietly dying in the stillness begin, slowly and then all at once, to grow.

I've been waiting to tell you this since Chapter 1.

Everything we've walked through — the Discover, the Define, the Develop — it was never just a career strategy. It was never just about purpose in the professional sense.

It's about your assignment.

I believe — based on everything I've seen, everything I've built, and twelve minutes *without breath in my body* that rearranged everything I thought I understood — that you are not here by accident. The specific set of gifts you carry, the specific experiences you've survived, the specific pain you know from the inside out — none of that is random.

It's a kit. Built for a specific job.

And when you figure out what that job is — when you stop running the performance and start running the mission — something shifts. Not just in your bank account. In your body. In the look on your face when Monday morning arrives.

A Divine Mandate, Not a Market Strategy

I want to be direct about where this mission comes from, because the origin matters more than most people expect it to. This is not a business strategy. It is not a gap identified in a market and decided to fill. It is not the product of research or competitive analysis or any process that began with what was profitable rather than what was true. This mission was given to me during twelve minutes when my body was on the wrong side of the line between here and gone—when my family stood around a hospital table and the question of whether I would come back was very real. I came back. And the clarity that arrived with me was this: there was work that only my particular DNA-driven purpose could do, work that would not exist in the world if I chose the comfortable path instead of the real one. The mission described in this book is that work. Not metaphorically. Literally.

Every person—every child who has been told their gifts are not practical, every adult who put their dreams in a drawer at twenty-two and forgot which drawer, every parent who gave everything to a life that fits everyone around them and no one inside them, every young person who is right now standing at the beginning of a road someone else built and wondering why it doesn't feel like theirs—deserves the chance to discover that the question of what they were born to do is not a luxury. It is not reserved for people with certain zip codes or certain last names or certain amounts of time and resources. It is the most fundamental human question, and it has an answer that was encoded in their DNA before the world had a single opportunity to tell them who to be instead.

The Invitation

Everything in this book has been building toward this single point. Not toward a conclusion—toward a beginning. Not toward a theory you agree with—toward a life you actually live. The three stages described across these chapters are not a framework you observe from the outside. They are an invitation to move through. Discover who you actually are beneath everything that was layered on top of you. Declare that person, out loud, in the choices you make starting today. Develop the life that expresses that person fully, in the economy, in your family, in the communities you inhabit—until the purpose that was written into your genetic design before you were born is finally, completely, unmistakably alive in the world.

The pond does not have to stay stagnant. The oxygen can return. The contribution that went quiet inside you does not have to stay quiet. The version of yourself that has been waiting—patient and encoded and entirely real—is not gone. It has been there the whole time, underneath everything, waiting for the exact moment when you decide that the costume is not worth what it costs and the real thing is not as impossible as it seemed.

One person steps into their purpose. Then another. Then the people who love them watch and ask the question for themselves. This is not a program selling you a transformation. This is a mirror showing you what was already true. The 1.5% is not a fixed number. It is an open door. And it has been open the entire time—not waiting for the right conditions, not waiting for the right season, not waiting for everything to line up or the fear to disappear.

Waiting for you. This is your time. Not someday. Now.

The Theory Was First. The Living Is Next.

You have been holding the theory. The framework. The full understanding of why 98.5% of people never close the gap between the life they are living and the life their DNA was designed to produce. You understand the three stages now—not as ideas to agree with, but as a process you are ready to move through.

Now comes the part that turns understanding into proof. And it happens in two directions at once.

Direction One: Your Daily Practice

The Step Into Success app is where the framework you just read comes alive in your actual life. Not in a weekend retreat. Not in a seminar that costs you three days and leaves you inspired but not equipped. In your daily life, in real time, in the moments between everything else that is already demanding your attention.

Inside the app, you will find guided tools for each stage of the Discover, Define, Develop process. Daily check-ins that ask the honest questions this book has been raising. Progress tracking that shows you, in plain terms, how far you have moved from where you started. And access to a community of people walking the same road—not to compare notes, but to confirm that the walk is real and the destination is worth every step.

Think of a seed. It knows what it was designed to become. But without the right soil, water, and light arranged around it—without the right conditions tended daily—it stays a seed. The Step Into Success app arranges the conditions. Every day. In small doses that protect the work against everything else competing for your time.

Street Translation: Knowing your purpose without a daily practice is like knowing where you want to go but never getting in the car. The app is the car. Get in.

visit:

<ins>https://sis-nashville.org</ins>

Direction Two: Where the Theory Takes You

This book is called Step Into Self: Theory for a reason. It handed you the map. It explained the terrain, named the obstacles, and showed you why the path matters. But there is a place on that map that this book pointed toward without fully entering. A place that lives on the other side of doing the work—not the work of reading about purpose, but the work of living from it.

That place has a name.

It is called the Purpose Level.

The next book in the Step Into Self series is built for the person who has done the work of Discover, made the declaration of Define, and is now in the daily grind of Develop—and needs to know what full DNA alignment actually looks and feels like when it is no longer a goal but a way of living. Not a destination you reach once and celebrate. A state you operate from. Every day. In your work, your relationships, your economics, and the legacy you leave behind.

Most people who read this book will feel the shift beginning. A few will act on it immediately. And the ones who stay with the process—who use the tools, do the daily work, and refuse to let the old life pull them back—will find themselves standing somewhere they could not have imagined from where they started.

91

That is where Purpose Level begins. Not where this book ends. Where the real life starts.

You have already started the climb. The next book is what waits at the top of the first hill—and shows you that what you thought was the summit is actually the beginning of the real terrain.

COMING NEXT:

PURPOSE LEVEL

The Next Book in the Step Into Self Series

By Raymond Williams

THE 24-HOUR CHECKPOINT

You have the theory. You have the vision. Now, you need the movement.

The greatest enemy of transformation isn't a lack of information—it's the waiting room. The 98.5% are always waiting for a sign, a permission slip, or a "better time" to start. But as we have discussed, your DNA doesn't wait for permission to grow. It simply follows its blueprint.

To cement your place in the 1.5%, I am giving you one final exercise. You must complete this within 24 hours of closing this book. Do not overthink it. Do not edit it. Just do it.

The DNA-Alignment Audit

Find a quiet space. Put away your phone. Grab a physical piece of paper and a pen. I want you to answer three questions with the honesty you'd give someone you actually trust—the kind that costs something to say out loud:

1. The Friction: What is the one area of your current life (work or personal) that feels most like a "costume" that doesn't fit? Where are you performing a role that is suffocating your spirit?

2. The Blueprint: If money were no longer a factor and fear was removed from the equation, what is the one thing you would do every day that makes you feel most alive, most useful, and most "at home" in your own skin?

3. The First Step: What is one "micro-move" you can make in the next 24 hours to honor that blueprint? (Examples: Making one phone call, researching one specific field, or writing down the work your DNA was designed to do).

I'm not asking you to quit your job by noon tomorrow. I'm asking you to stop lying to yourself. Identifying the friction is the first step toward the ripple. Once you name the lie, the truth starts to take over.

The Promise

When you take that first step, the DNA that has been waiting starts to move. The fog begins to thin. You aren't just reading a book anymore—you are reclaiming your identity. The stone does not ask the lake for permission before it drops. It just drops. And the ripple follows.

Always.

One day, or Day One. You decide.

THE CONCLUSION

There is a version of you that has been waiting for this moment since the day you were born.

It isn't a "better" version of you. You're not a richer or more famous version. You are simply the aligned version. You are the person who has finally stopped fighting your own design and started living out the purpose written into your DNA by the Architect of the Universe.

You have spent these chapters looking at the math. You know now that 98.5% of the world is sleepwalking. They are good people, but they are living in a fog of "shoulds" and "supposed-tos." They are paying a debt they never signed for, chasing a success that doesn't belong to them.

We have explored the structural necessity of Professional Economics© and the deep-seated transformation of the Edification of Education©. We have laid the theoretical foundation for a life of staggering, almost unimaginable impact.

But the theory is over now. The book is almost closed. What matters now isn't what you know—it's who you are going to be when you set this down. Are you going back to the fog, or are you stepping into the light?

Imagine you are standing at the edge of a vast, stagnant lake. For years, you've been told that the stillness is "safety." But I am telling you that the stillness is death. You are the stone. Your decision to live your DNA-driven purpose is the ripple. When you hit the water, the lake changes. The waves move outward. They touch the shore. They move the earth. You were never meant to just take up space; you were meant to change the frequency of the water.

Without breath in my body for twelve minutes after my heart forgot how to beat. I saw the edge. And I can tell you with the conviction of a man who has died and returned: the only thing that will matter when you reach that edge is whether or not you used the gift you were given.

You weren't an accident. Your passions aren't a mistake. Your DNA is a divine mandate.

The 98.5% are waiting for a leader. Your family is waiting for a father who is truly alive. The world is waiting for the specific, irreplaceable contribution that only you can make.

The door is open. The ladder is down. The DNA is ready.

Stop doing. Start being. Step into self. Don't just live a life. Be the life you were born to live.

YOUR NEXT STEP

The book is closed. The work is open.

If something in these pages shifted in you—even slightly, even just a crack in something that had been sealed for a long time—do not let that shift settle back into the old shape. The resistance will try. It always does. The fog will try to roll back in. The old life will try to look more comfortable than it felt before you read this. That is normal. That is not a sign you are losing the ground you found. It is a sign that you found real ground and something noticed.

Here is what you do with the shift.

First: Take the 24-Hour Checkpoint seriously. Go back to it right now if you skipped past it. Do the three questions. Write them on real paper with a real pen. Name the friction that has been costing you. Name the blueprint that has been waiting. Name the one micro-move you can make before tomorrow comes. Then make it. Not someday. Today. The stone does not ask the lake for permission before it drops.

Second: Download the Step Into Success app. The framework that lives in this book now needs to live in your daily routine. Five minutes a day. The digging, the declaring, the developing—done consistently, in small doses, in the real conditions of your real life. That is how the shift becomes permanent. That is how the 98.5% becomes the 1.5%.

Third: Know that there is more on the other side of this. Purpose Level—the next book in this series—is being written for exactly the person you are becoming right now. The person who did not just read about transformation but started living it. The book you are holding was the theory. The next one is about what it feels like when the theory becomes the truth of how you wake up every single morning.

You were not an accident. Your gifts are not a mistake. The purpose written into your DNA before the world had a chance to tell you who to be instead—it has not expired. It has been waiting. It is still waiting. And after everything in these pages, you now know that the waiting is a choice. Not a fate.

TAKE THE NEXT STEP RIGHT NOW

Step Into Success App

www.sis-nashville.org

Coming Next:

PURPOSE LEVEL

The Next Book in the Step Into Self Series

www.sis-nashville.org

One day, or Day One.

You already decided.

Raymond Williams: The Architect of DNA-Driven Purpose

*Raymond Williams doesn't just teach transformation; he is the living proof of it. A Nashville native, proud father, and grateful son, Raymond spent three decades climbing the ladders of professional success, accumulating the degrees and high-level certifications—from **DISC Master Behavioral Specialist** to **Executive Coach**—that the world told him defined his worth. But his true mission wasn't born in a classroom or a boardroom. It was forged in the profound, harrowing silence of twelve minutes without breath in my body—twelve minutes where the line between "here" and "gone" blurred, and the titles and credentials stripped away.*

*When Raymond came back, he brought with him a fierce, undeniable clarity: most people are performing a version of success that doesn't fit them. He realized that true power resides in the purpose written into our **DNA** before we were old enough to fight it. This revelation birthed the **Step Into Self** framework—a precision tool designed not for motivation, but for the deep, honest excavation of one's original intent.*

*Through his work across healthcare, government, and the C-suite, Raymond challenges leaders to stop wearing the "costume" of their roles and start leading from their truth. Yet, his greatest legacy is lived at home. By aligning his life with his DNA-encoded purpose, he models for his children what it looks like to stop performing and start living. Whether he is mentoring the next generation through **Professional Concepts Services** and **Step Into Success**, or guiding an executive through a career pivot, Raymond's message is singular and soulful: The lie ends here. Your purpose is not a luxury—it is your blueprint. It's time to step into who you were always meant to be.*

Step Into Success Programs: www.sis-nashville.org

The transformation doesn't end on the last page. The Step Into Success app turns the theory of this book into an actionable blueprint—for students, parents, and educators alike—by mapping your unique personality DNA and aligning it with your future.

5 REASONS TO START YOUR ASSESSMENT TODAY

1. **Personality DNA Blueprint — For All Ages**

   DISC Assessments tailored for every life stage—Kids, Youth, Adults, Re-entry, and Leadership. Discover what motivates you, how you handle conflict, and how to communicate with clarity.

2. **Gamified Growth: The Robot Factory — For Kids**

   Kids build their personality profile in an interactive "Robot Factory." Their custom robot dances, lights up, and levels up—making self-discovery fun and age appropriate.

3. **Career Alignment & Future Mapping — For Youth**

   Bridge the gap between "Who am I?" and "What should I do?" The Youth Career Explorer matches your DISC results to career paths that fit your natural strengths.

4. **Tools for Educators & Parents**

   The Teacher Dashboard lets you assign modules, access the Resource Center, and use the Training Manual to lead deeper conversations about purpose, behavior, and potential.

5. **Full Reports & Team Building**

   Download a Comprehensive Full Report and use the Teams feature to compare profiles with family or colleagues—building stronger, more empathetic relationships.

READY TO STEP INTO SUCCESS?

Scan the code or visit us online to unlock your free assessment and start your journey toward a purpose-driven life.

www.SIS-Nashville.org

One day, or Day One. You decide.